STUMBLING
THROUGH
LIFE

STUMBLING THROUGH LIFE

(A Memoir)

BILL DOMJAN

In Memory of Frank Springer

(1929-2009)

Good friend, good neighbor and verbal sparring partner
over all things political

Table of Contents

FORWARD

Although born in Brooklyn on May 9, 1932, - it was Mother's Day - I was raised in Queens, New York (Richmond Hill for my first five years, Hollis for the next seven years and Rosedale from the time I was 12 years old till 19). The U.S. Army for three years from 1951 to 54, Hofstra College for two years and then Brooklyn Polytech for another two plus. Went to work for the Sperry Gyroscope Company from 1959 till 1965 and then to Grumman Aviation to work on the Apollo Space Program. I earned my Master's Degree in System Science from Brooklyn Poly in 1969. Laid off from Grumman in 1974 and went back to work for Sperry till 1989 when I left for Parsons Brinckerhoff. Married Barbara Blatnicky in 1963 and had three children: Stephen, 1964; Joseph 1965; and Bobbi, 1967. Sounds simple and straightforward, but like most people there is a story to be told that cannot be expressed by a mere listing of names, times and dates.

Over the years I have heard tales from Barbara's parents (now deceased) and other folks from my previous generation, and have always wished the information had been recorded in some way. Old photos provide clues to the past of our family's lives, and although it is said one picture is worth a thousand words, they sometimes only provide a tantalizing glimpse of what has been. There are times when words are required.

I never thought about adding anything to the historical record until a few years ago when my daughter-in-law, Pamela, asked me to put in writing something about my life. I am sure she wanted something for her two young boys to be able to remember their grandparents by. Now there are books that provide an outline for supplying this information and include spaces for date of birth, schools attended, marriage(s), divorce(s), children and all the other statistical data that defines a life. But that is really just a two dimensional picture that can be described in the first paragraph of this Forward. But, how would you define the real you?

I tried to write a chronological history of my life but it reminded me of reading a high school history text. Dates followed facts to be remembered for tests, but afterwards were soon forgotten. There was no life to it. I said to myself, I can write a memoir, but nobody will read it.

Instead, I decided to write a short essay about my school days, from grade school through college (it is the first essay in this book). That was over ten years ago and it did not read badly, so I wrote another one, this time about my three years in the army. And then another and another. I have over thirty now and they add up to almost 200 pages. Some cover relatively long periods of time, like the different schools I attended with their successes and failures, and others just a brief incident like my bicycle ride to work on the first Earth Day in 1970. In these little vignettes, I try to include what everyday life was like at the time.

The essays do not really add up to a legitimate memoir but they do give a glimpse into my life and times over the years. I have tried to recall events that may be of passing interest to my family, friends and hopefully my grandkids. It is rather disjointed, as has been my life. That is why the title. I have managed to stumble through life for over seven decades. Valedictorian one year, school dropout the next. Land a job – lose a job. Try to fly – crash land.

Bill Domjan 2010

SCHOOL DAYS

Reading, writing and stumbling

S chool has been a mixed experience for me. Valedictorian in grammar school, high school dropout, busted in the U. S. Army for playing hooky in training school, Dean's List in freshman year at Hofstra College, failed in senior year at Brooklyn Polytech (job offer rescinded from Republic Aircraft) and eventually got graduate degree from Poly (took six years for five year program). Now for a little explanation.

At 12 years old, my mother died and within a year my father remarried. We moved from St. Albans, where I was a good student in an excellent school, to Rosedale where I became an excellent student in a good but not excellent school. As a result I was the valedictorian of my class and entered Brooklyn Technical High School, one of three public schools in New York City that required passing an entrance test for admission. However, my attitude toward education did not last. At 14 my father died, and my sister and I continued to live with our stepmother who then had a nervous breakdown. It was an unhappy household.

I was going to Tech, spending three hours a day commuting (a bus and two subway rides) while my friends were busy playing basketball in the afternoons. School did not interest me, I cut classes and occasionally would continue past my school stop (Fulton St. on the GG Local) and go on to Manhattan with my good friend Jack Reynolds (a student at St. Francis Prep with a similar attitude toward school). With our lunch money we would stop at Nedick's (Nickel Nick Nedick's – Eat Well and Save Money Too) where ten cents would get us a small orange drink, coffee and a doughnut (this was around 1950). The New York Paramount Theater was $.55 before one o'clock. (Frank Sinatra was just starting his singing career with all the "bobbysoxer's" swooning at his Paramount Theater performances.)

My singular claim to academic fame was taking Dick Crowel's geometry regents (made $5.00 and got him a grade of 96.) However, many of my personal test grades were less than 65 and after four and a half years of high school, I still needed another term of English to graduate. It was February 1951, the Korean War was being fought, and most of my friends were going into the service. So I joined the army

I was in the paratroopers and aside from the occasional thrill of jumping out of a plane (did it 25 times) it was the most boring period of my life. Although I did have an exciting experience when I dove off a bridge on a $5 bet. (See "You're in the Army Now" for the details)

Aside from learning how to jump out of an airplane, I did have one other educational experience. While attending Field Wireman training at Fort Jackson, South Carolina I found the classes so dull that I would go to the base library instead. I got caught there one day and was immediately busted from Corporal to Private First Class. After completing training (going to all of the remaining interminably boring classes), I returned to my home base at Fort Benning, Georgia somewhat embarrassed at my demotion.

I also took a home study English course and on a leave took the NYS English regents (grade 66).

Discharged in February 1954, I came back to New York needing some place to live and wondering what I would do with myself. My stepmother had moved back to the Bronx (there never was any thought of going back into that household), my friends all lived in Rosedale, and I decided to live in the YMCA in Jamaica, Queens. I had a thousand dollars when discharged and proceeded to buy a car – a 1951 Henry J – the absolutely worst car ever built. Henry J. Kaiser had built Liberty ships during the Second World War and was able to produce a freighter from keel laying to completed ship in 30 days. The Henry J, built at a time when there was a high demand for cars must have been built in 30 minutes. $500 of worthless junk that continually needed repairs.

Aptitude test

But I now had a place to live and a car to drive – what next? Well, one of my veteran's benefits was to take a special aptitude test that would evaluate my educational and vocational abilities. Recommendations would be provided on what type of job or further education should be pursued - even job placement for those with special abilities. I took the test, which included both written and manual sections, and later sat down with an adviser to review the results. They told me I had very good academic potential and should think about going to college. Also, I had the conceptual ability to visualize the final configuration of something, given a number of component parts. They would even find a position for me that would take advantage of these superior skills, until I could pursue a higher education. I did not know what this all meant, but it sure sounded good; a great job followed by acceptance into one of the finer educational institutions. However, my expectations were soon dashed. The resulting job in the Garret Belt factory was to take shipping orders for different numbers of belts, and judge what size carton to place them in. It was 1954, the pay was $1.00 per hour and I wasn't making enough to live on. So much for aptitude tests.

How to build a house

While working at the belt factory my stepmother's brother, Al, asked if I would help him build a house in Croton-on-the-Hudson during a one-month vacation he was about to take. The pay would be minimal, we would work seven days a week from sunup to sundown and he would cover all living expenses.

It was one of life's great experiences!

When we arrived, the footings had been poured and that is about all. Al had bought a book on how to build a house, got a relatively simple set of plans for a summer cape, had materials delivered to the site, got himself a helper (me) and started to build. And build we did. We stayed at a nearby motel, and each evening during dinner, we would go over the plans for the next day's work. Sills were placed over the footings, rough flooring laid, and walls framed. Each morning we would rise early, eat, and head to the site where we would be busy the entire day. Each evening – exhausted – we would eat, plan, sleep and then start all over. To witness this pile of lumber metamorphose into a building was pure magic. And Al and I were responsible for this. But it wasn't magic, it was just the result of something reasonably well planned and then executed with tenacity. At the end of the month the house was completely framed, windows and doors installed, and fully sheathed. It even looked like a house!

It is kind of strange but I never went back to see that house again. In fact that was my last contact with any of my stepmother's family.

College bound

It was during this same period that I decided to go to college. Belt factory work was not the way to fame and fortune. My problem was, how does one go about getting into college? (I was now a high school graduate having recently picked up my Brooklyn Tech diploma – seven and a half years in the making.) Even more basic was what school to go to? There were no guidance counselors to turn to and most of my friends were not going to college. The only thing I knew was that many of the kids at Brooklyn Tech, my old high school, had talked about going to Brooklyn Polytech. So there I went, in person, only to find out that a transcript of my marks was required along with an official application. When they eventually received my transcript with its low average and long list of failed subjects, I was politely but firmly rejected. However, I was told Polytech had a working agreement with Hofstra College, in Hempstead Long Island, and that upon satisfactory completion of two years of pre-engineering there, Polytech would accept me for the final two years. Next stop, Hofstra.

I drove out to the school, filled out an application, submitted my high school transcript and waited to hear from them. At that time Hofstra College was a relatively small school looking to expand and they were willing to accept me on a non-matriculated basis for the fall semester.

Summer ended and I started Hofstra in the fall of 1954. The school placement office had listings of places to stay and jobs to be had. I took one of each. The living arrangements were a furnished room in a private home in nearby Hempstead Village. The owner was a nice middle-aged lady who told me I had the run of the house. However, my room was at the top of the stairs, next to the hall bathroom, and that was just about all that I ever saw of the place. I never felt comfortable there and felt even more uncomfortable when hearing her amorously cavorting downstairs with her occasional men friends. Studying was pretty much done at school.

The bowling alley

The job was at Tulip Hill Lanes, a bowling alley in Floral Park, about five miles from the school. I worked as a pinboy three or four nights a week; in those days there were no automatic pinsetters. When pins had to be reset, a treadle was stepped on by the pinboy causing steel pegs to stick up from the alley at the correct pin locations. The pins had holes in the bottom allowing them to be placed at the correct spots. Stoop, pick up pins, place them on pegs; stoop, pick up pins, place them on pegs - it was hard work and it was boring.

Since doing so poorly in high school and being rejected by Brooklyn Polytech, there was a strong incentive to get good grades. And I did – at least at first. They were A's and B's and I was soon a

7

matriculated student (I even made the Dean's list one semester.) The G.I. Bill was covering most of my tuition expenses and I almost made enough to live on. Never gave too much thought to money and to paraphrase today's ball players I was taking it just "one semester at a time."

At the end of my freshman year it didn't appear I'd have enough money to continue into my second year. Fortunately the three owners of the bowling alley (Joe Tapfar, Harry Holland and Jim Deegan) offered me a deal. I would clean the bowling alley each day and receive room and board in return. The room would be the bowling alley (after the end of bowling each night I would take a rollaway bed out of a closet and sleep next to the alleys) and board was whatever was available in their small kitchen (usually the blue plate special – a burger and fries). It was a good deal and I accepted; it looked like I would be getting through my second year of school.

That summer (1955) I moved into Tulip Hill Lanes. The bowling alley was on two levels and my "bedroom" was on the second floor – it was six alleys wide. (I would later brag that I had the largest bedroom on Long Island.) Little did I realize that I would be sharing this new home with my predecessor – Louie LaBuff. Louie was a scrawny red haired kid about my age (twenty something) who had been cleaning the place, but was fired because he did such a poor job. However, Joe Tapfar felt sorry for him and let him stay there. (He would probably be one of the homeless today.) He never rated a bed like me (I guess that was reserved for the college-bound homeless) and slept on the bowling alley benches. Louie was a character; he lived for bowling, and money earned setting pins was just about all spent on bowling. In fact the first thing he did upon arising from his bench each morning was to throw a bowling ball down the alley. He was a little guy who would undress and bathe in a basin of warm water on the kitchen table while people would be cooking. In retrospect it probably wasn't a bad idea as I was using the men's room to take cold sponge baths whenever necessary (probably didn't smell too good those days).

One night Louie and I had a fight over something and the alley owners threw him out. He had been living there on borrowed time and this little incident triggered that action.

When not studying at school I would retreat to the basement and underneath a hanging light bulb, next to the beer kegs, I would sit at an old table and hit the books. As a joke some of my homework assignments were done on the back of old paper place mats.

One night, after the bowlers had left, after I had pulled out the rollaway from the closet and after I was sound asleep, the local police officer did a routine check of the bowling alley front door. It was unlocked. Shortly after, I was awakened by someone roughly shaking my shoulder and saying, "Who are you and what are you doing here?" I was startled by the shaking and blinded by the bright flashlight beam in my eyes. After eventually realizing who was there, I explained my situation and was allowed to go back to sleep. For a long time afterward it was a big joke among all the locals, how Bill the bartender had forgotten to lock the door when he closed the place (Bill was known to have one or two or three for the road before calling it a night) and the resulting early morning interrogation.

Floral Park friends

It was while working at Tulip Hill I met Bob Johnson, a young man my age who recently moved to Floral Park with his folks after a four-year stint as a hard-hat diver in the U.S. Navy. Mr. and Mrs. Johnson were born in Sweden and all eight of their children were the outdoor type. But most of all Bob, who was a real miniature Viking. At 5' 3" he had red hair, the shoulders of a linebacker, and athletic ability I envied. We became good friends – I became part of his extended family – and got involved in many activities. This included joining the Republican Recruits, who met every Wednesday at Koenig's Restaurant. We knew or cared nothing about politics at that time but were interested in meeting young girls, and there were plenty in this club. There was very little politics involved and every month one of the other local

Republican Recruit clubs would sponsor a dance that was always well attended.

Bob and I would also play tennis – he was good, I was not – and occasionally go skiing when we got a few dollars together. We would use Bob's ski equipment.

A brief word about Bob's ski equipment that was representative of the time. In his basement was a barrel of old wooden skis; they were called "hickories" and for good reason. They were solid wood with edges made of small one foot sections of steel about a quarter inch wide and screwed into the edges of the skis (there were many times while skiing that one of the segments would come loose and the remedy was to just pull the whole piece off and screw it back later). The ski bindings were called "bear traps" because when the boot toe was strapped to the ski and the grooved heel held in place by a cable, they looked like bear traps. And they didn't release when your leg twisted in a fall - never.

Next to the barrel of skis was a pile of ski boots; at that time boots looked a lot like work shoes except the toe was square and the heel had a groove around the side so it could be held in place by the ski binding's cable mechanism. Bob's basement also had a collection of bamboo poles of varying length with huge baskets (designed for support in deep powder snow).

This equipment had been used over the years by Bob and his seven brothers and sisters and various other relatives who had been skiing long before it had become a mainstream sport.

We would try to find two skis of equal length, boots close to our size (and the same size as each other) and two poles about the same length (baskets could be of different diameter). Then off to the slopes. Many times this was Fahnstock State Park, a small T-bar area right on the Taconic Parkway about two hours from home.

It was also at the bowling alley that I met Mickey Walsh. Mickey collected the Tulip Hill garbage, but he was no ordinary garbage man. He and his father, a 300-pound hard drinking Irishman, had their own small garbage collection route in nearby Bellrose Terrace. (There were stories of Big Jim throwing fellow patrons through plate glass barroom windows and of carrying a loaded shotgun in the truck when unions threatened to organize him.) Mickey was an avid boatman, lived on a canal in Massapequa and occasionally I would work on the truck with him to make a few extra dollars. It was there I learned the garbage man's song –"Put out your can, here comes the garbage man".

But I digress. Back to school. My sophomore year at Hofstra went relatively smoothly – going to classes, studying, working and even doing some beer drinking and socializing. However, in addition to setting pins I was now responsible for cleaning the bowling alley and occasionally worked as bartender. I would be up at 6:30 AM and start sweeping the bar. I even tried watching Sunrise Semester on the TV so I would be learning while earning. Except they were very bookish programs which I didn't understand

I was also doing a poor job of cleaning the place - so poor, I was fired at the end of the 1956 school year and they hired someone else. Strangely enough, with the firing came an improvement in my living conditions.

Apartment living (with Eddie)

The Tulip Hill Lanes were in a two story brick building on the corner of Tulip Avenue (a main road that ran through the center of Floral Park) and Hill St. (a residential street). On the first floor there was a bar and eight bowling alleys and on the second level were six more alleys (my bedroom) and two small apartments. Jim Deegan and his family lived in one apartment, and one room of the other apartment was used as an office for the business. The three partners thought it might be a good idea to use this apartment to provide their next janitor with a real place to live (maybe they could get someone more reliable). And as long as they were opening up the apartment for the new help, why not let me move in too. I was still working as a pinboy, doing an occasional stint as bartender, filling in as manager and helping out doing odd jobs as needed. So my good deal got better; I would even be able to take a hot shower and go to bed before bowling ended. However, there was one hitch (the Yin and the Yang you might say). My janitorial replacement and fellow apartment-mate would be Eddie.

Eddie was a good-looking guy, muscular (a body builder), well spoken with a deep resonant voice (he sounded like he could have been a radio announcer) and about 30 years old. Why did he take such a menial job? Why were his previous jobs as bedpan jockies in nursing homes and hospitals? One reason - he was crazy.

In casual conversations Ed sounded quite sane, being reasonably well informed and articulate in his speech. However beneath the surface he was nuts. Ed claimed that priests had made sexual advances toward him, slept with a knife under his pillow for protection, was concerned that he would be attacked by mad dogs in the streets and thought that people who rode motorcycles were the modern equivalent of the Wild West's cowboys.

One night in the bowling alley kitchen he mentioned something about Eisenhower, who was then president. I countered with a rather innocuous remark like. "I don't believe that" and he became enraged. With eyes bulging he picked up a long kitchen knife and came after me saying, "Are you calling me a liar?" The two owners there were dumbstruck. I was just plain scared. For a few short seconds nobody knew what was going to happen. However, Eddie - realizing what he was doing - managed to return to normalcy, saying he was only kidding. The rest of us knew otherwise. After this I believe the partners were afraid to fire Ed and I was careful what I said to him.

Brooklyn Polytech

The fall of 1956 would be the start of my junior year in college and I would be going to the Polytechnic Institute of Brooklyn, the institute that rejected me two years earlier. I would show 'em. I didn't.

Polytech was a problem for me. I had proven to myself I could pass college engineering courses if I put my mind to it, but now I was losing my motivation. Part of it was the long commute to Brooklyn, then finding a parking space and then the long ride home. I did not take part in school activities and it seemed to be a repeat of my unsuccessful high school days at Brooklyn Tech. Another part was that my social life was picking up – going to local dances most Friday nights and to Republican Recruit meetings at Koenig's Restaurant right in Floral Park each Wednesday evening. These usually turned into big nights of beer drinking and my Thursday classes suffered.

I continued going to Polytech, but my motivation was diminishing with each semester. I was living more for each day, with little planning for tomorrow. In a rut, I continued with school, going through the motions, sitting in classes trying to stay awake and barely paying attention. My grades were poor, but I did manage to pass all courses through my junior year and the first half of my senior year. Then it all caught up with me.

The marketplace for engineers in 1958 was not great, but I did manage to receive a job offer from Republic Aircraft in Farmingdale, starting right after graduation. (Little did I realize that graduation would not occur in 1958.) That spring, two of my instructors in the Aero department (that was my major) got together and decided that my grades were too low to award me a degree. So they collectively failed me in the subjects I was taking with them.

I was devastated. I lost my job and had to continue with my part time work at the bowling alley, along with working occasionally for Mickey Walsh on the garbage truck (there was no lilt in my voice when singing the garbage man's song that summer). There was a lesson to be learned from my folly, but it would not be until 14 years later, at 40 years old, that the lesson would sink in. "Life may be a crapshoot in some respects, but you tend to get what you deserve in the long run".

Fortunately, that fall Sperry hired me as an engineering-aid, at a half decent salary, and I started my professional career. In the spring of 1959 I returned to Poly (night school) and satisfactorily completed my two courses. I now had a bachelor's degree in aeronautical engineering and was promoted to engineer at Sperry.

My formal education did not end there however. Although I never liked school there was something inside telling me to continue on. And I did just that. My first crack at graduate school was at Adelphi College (now university) taking two advanced physics courses. I did not have the vaguest idea what they were about and my idea for a graduate physics degree quickly vaporized. Next was my attempt at a Master's degree in System Science back at Brooklyn Poly. They now had a graduate school in Farmingdale, Sperry would pay the tuition, and classes were right after work.

It was 1963, I had just married and school started right after returning from my honeymoon. In general, classes were held two nights a week with most of my studying during lunch hour. Six years and three kids later I received my degree. I was 37 years old and finally no longer had that strange masochistic desire to struggle through any more technical courses. There would be other things to learn, some requiring formal training and others learned on my own. Some I was successful in (sailing small boats and windsurfing) and others I failed (snowboarding and flying).

I have learned/stumbled along life's road.

A STORY ABOUT TEETH

I visit the dentist for repair and maintenance of my teeth on a regular basis. It was not always that way.

R ecently I brushed my teeth with something other than toothpaste. But let me begin somewhat earlier - about a half century earlier. I was born in 1932 and grew up during World War II. My father was an air raid warden and although we never had an air raid, I remember studying the silhouettes of the German Heinkel, Stuka and Messerschmitt bombers. I also remember that toothpaste came in soft metal tubes made mostly of tin. As the toothpaste was used, the end of the tube was squeezed and rolled up, where it stayed in that position (by looking you always knew how much paste was left in the tube). When finished, it was recycled along with tin cans, cooking grease and newspapers.

When the war ended so did my tooth brushing although there was no connection. I also avoided going to the dentist, as I would sooner have my toenails removed. Those were the days when a trip to the dentist was preceded by days of fear and terror. Drills were low speed and hot, the dentist leaned heavily on the drill and Novocain was rarely given. The pain was unimaginable and I did not go often. Cavities got bigger and more numerous and after joining the army in 1951- still without a high school diploma – Uncle Sam's dentists decided it was easier to yank a few teeth rather than repair them. My two front teeth remained, but two on one side and one on the other were replaced by plastic teeth on a removable upper plate. For the next forty years I rinsed my mouth after every meal, as food would get stuck between the plate and the roof of my mouth. But that is not the point of the story.

Water Skiing

One time when water skiing in Long Island's Great South Bay, an amazing event occurred. I was with some friends on their boat and had with me on a first date a very sophisticated young lady, Brenda O'Sullivan (she later married a U.S. Congressman from Garden City). Needless to say I was trying to make an impression on Brenda by exhibiting my water skiing skills – jumping the wake, skiing on one ski, and performing other sophomoric stunts. In the process I took a rather hard fall on my face, which normally is no big deal – it's only water – but my mouth was open and my teeth fell out. Now although the water is only about four feet deep, the bottom is soft and mucky; anything falling to the bottom quickly sinks into the mud.

I figured soft food would be my diet for a while. Also, with my Bugs Bunny appearance this would probably be my last date with the fair Lady Brenda. There was only one chance in a million that my plate would be found. However, there must have been 999,999 sets of teeth lost in the Great South Bay, because Joe Miro, while searching the area, felt something with his toes, in the muck and mire that turned out to be my plastic teeth. Brenda never had to see me in my "What's up Doc" role and we even went out again a few more times.

Saratoga Springs

There is a saying that what goes around comes around - and that is just what happened. Although Joe Miro lived on Long Island, his parents had a motel in Saratoga Springs in Upstate New York, and about a year later a few of us went with Joe to visit his folks. It just so happens that Joe's mom is an excellent cook and she made us a delicious Italian dinner that first night that I could not stop eating. You might say my stomach was bigger than my eyes.

After dinner, being young and virile, we went off to tour the local bars "looking for action". The action consisted of hoisting many glasses of beer, and when we eventually returned to the motel my head was spinning and my belly was about to burst. In the middle of the night with my stomach churning madly and overcome with nausea, I stumbled into the bathroom, threw up my guts and flushed the toilet. I had also thrown up something else – my teeth. Joe had giveth me my teeth and now he had taketh them away.

Although I had a pretty dopey smile without my teeth and whistled a little when talking, I figured if I did not smile and talked carefully I could get away with it for a while. Little did I realize that people were saying, "I guess Bill was in an accident while driving his stock car". Eventually I got another set of teeth.

The Blue Angel

Then I met my wife-to-be, Barbara. We had been seeing each other for a time but she had no idea that I was not whole. Just prior to a date that would take us to New York City to see Phyllis Diller at the Blue Angel, I broke my plate while chewing some hard candy. This required immediate action, so I visited my friend down the street, Bob Johnson. He was familiar with using fiberglass and epoxy resin to repair boats and car bodies. Teeth couldn't be that different – or could they? We would soon find out.

Bob mixed some epoxy and hardener, soaked a small piece of fiberglass in the mixture and then applied it to the two pieces of my plate. It sure looked like it was working. It might be a little big in my mouth but it would be better than nothing.

The only problem was that I was going out that night with Barbara and it did not appear to be hardening fast enough. Well, Bob said that if we applied a little heat the process could be quickened. A hair dryer did the job in just a few minutes but left us (us? - me) with somewhat of a problem. The teeth had warped and I could not get my

17

mouth closed. I tried and tried, and eventually got it closed but only after breaking the denture again. It appeared I would have to try to talk carefully and try not to smile.

That night I picked up Barbara, met Bob Martin (who would eventually become my best man) and his wife Ginny, and off we went to the city. I never mentioned my problem to anyone, and thought I could get away with it if I spoke slowly and covered my mouth when smiling. I was mistaken.

We grabbed a bite to eat before the show and when asked about dessert I said, "I'll have some. You know me and my sweet tooth". Bob calmly responded, "Bill, you seem to have left your sweet tooth home this evening". I laugh about it now, but at the time I felt like a first class jerk.

Maine Canoe Trip

Another time, while in the wilds of Maine, on a weeklong canoe trip with the Boy Scouts I had another misadventure. A guide, ten boys (including my two sons) and I were camped on the riverbank for the night and before retiring to my tent I brushed my teeth. In the process, I removed my bridge, placed it in a small cup of water, brushed my real teeth and then emptied the cup into the shallow water next to shore. I then blissfully went to sleep, being very tired from a tough day of paddling (my tongue was apparently so tired it did not notice that it had a lot more room to move around in my mouth). The next morning my son Stephen was standing at the river's edge and happened to see something familiar looking up at him from below the surface. "Dad, look what I found". He has been telling the story ever since.

However, the saga does not end there. At my regular visits to the dentist, Dr. Adler would always ask me when I was going to replace my flapper with a permanent bridge. I was so accustomed to these teeth that it did not seem worth the bother or expense. Then when about 60 years old, I was in a local theater production and had a few lines to say ("Hark is that a cannon I hear?" – an old joke). A few days before opening night my plate broke again. I was panic-stricken. How could I say my lines. Not only would I look like Bugs Bunny, but without my teeth I would sound like Elmer Fudd. I called Dr. Adler and although the office was closed he agreed to make a temporary repair. And temporary it was. It lasted through my four performances and then broke again. This time I agreed to have a permanent bridge installed and I have had it ever since with no problems. Actually there is one problem; there are no more stories to tell about my teeth except for the one that started this tale.

Toothpaste

And now getting back to where my story began – about toothpaste and toothpaste tubes. Along with my habits, toothpaste containers have changed over the years. No longer are they made of soft foil that easily rolls up, but rather of ubiquitous plastic with various means of extraction. Tubes that easily squeeze, pumps that extrude three different colors and little semi-rigid bottles that defy emptying unless pounded vigorously to get the paste near the exit. It was the latter that Barbara had bought and each day I would battle to get that damn paste onto my toothbrush. Then one morning I noticed a squeeze tube on the sink that had obviously replaced the cantankerous plastic bottle. I squeezed, the toothpaste came out easily and I thought to myself, Barbara has finally listened to my complaints. However, the stuff tasted awful and as I continued to brush my teeth, thought to myself, when will she ever get it together and buy decent tasting toothpaste in a useable dispenser. I complained to her later and she said she had not bought any new toothpaste. I insisted there was new toothpaste. She said no. Later, after investigating, she laughed while telling me, "that was not toothpaste, it was hair gel". The Moral: don't brush your teeth without first putting on your glasses.

ROSEDALE

At twelve years old, I moved to Rosedale. The seven years spent there greatly influenced the rest of my life.

Rosedale (early ads for homes called it the rising community on the Sunrise) was my home as a teenager from 1944 to 1951. The world was different then and Rosedale was different from the rest of the world. By day, the center of activity for the teens was Brookville Park. It was about a mile long, a quarter mile wide, had baseball fields, a lake with row boats, walking paths and even some tennis courts (although none of us would even think of playing such a sissy sport). However, the absolute center of attraction at Brookville Park was the basketball courts. Our whole lives seemed to revolve around this game. It was a white man's sport then, and our heroes were the New York Knicks with Ernie Vanderweigh, Carl Braun, and Harry Gallatin. Field goals were shot with two hands and Bob Cousy was the star of the Andrew Jackson High School team where many Rosedale kids went (I went to Brooklyn Tech which I hated because the long commute kept me from playing basketball in the afternoon). There was always a game going on and when within earshot of the court you would yell, "I have winners". School and the blackness of night were the only things that kept us from playing our half-court games. Rain and snow just slowed us down a little.

Nights were spent hanging out in front of the two candy stores in town: Pete's and Murray Sweigenbaum's. Television was in its infancy and most of our families did not have sets. We were a little too old to sit around with our parents in the evening and it really was not the kind of community where anyone was encouraged to do homework, so we hung around the candy stores. If you smoked, Pete would sell you "loosie" cigarettes at a penny each (all the big name athletes and celebrities endorsed cigarettes - Arthur Godfrey the popular radio host endorsed Chesterfields for years until he had a cancerous lung removed). Out on the sidewalk, we would pitch pennies up against the wall; closest to the wall won. On that same wall we would play Chinese handball and when the ball hit the point where the wall met the sidewalk it was a do-over and was called a hindu. That same sidewalk had a third use – crap shooting.

Let's shoot craps

One Saturday evening, hanging around in front of Pete's candy store, Walter Tinney, Joey Miro and I decided to go to the movies. A double feature (all the theaters showed two full-length films, plus news, coming attractions and a cartoon) was at the Garden Theater (in Springfield Gardens) just a short nickel bus ride away. Although the movie tickets were only 35 cents each, our pooled resources were not enough to make the show.

Joe suggested we use his 7-Up dice to beat someone out of the additional money needed for our evening's entertainment. The dice were souvenirs from the 7-Up company, with one die having five spots on each face and the other all two's, so a seven appeared on every roll. If we could get someone to bet against the roller we would win on the first roll with a guaranteed seven. The only potential problem was that the die with all twos had one face with the word **Up** on it. There would be one chance in six that when the dice were rolled the **Up** would appear and our scheme exposed.

At about that time Howie Holland (a tough, older teenager who we were afraid of) swaggered up to the corner and said, "What are you

21

guys doin?" It took a lot of courage, but Walt said, "Shootin' crap, wanna play Howie?" "Yeah", said Howie. Bets were made, money laid on the sidewalk, Howie betting against Joe who would be rolling the dice. It was getting dark so it probably wouldn't be noticed that one die was all fives and the other all twos. But what if the **Up** appeared? Howie would kill us.

As Joe was shaking the dice preparing to roll, Walt and I were shaking in our shoes. We held our breaths – Joe rolled and as the dice tumbled across the sidewalk we prayed we would be going to the movies and not the hospital. Seven - without the **Up** – appeared! Then, as I said, "The bus is coming, we have to leave, so long Howie", Joe scooped up the money and we all high-tailed it for the bus. There are times when crime does pay.

Let's have a drink

Rosedale was a blue-collar community. Many of the fathers were New York City cops or firemen and regulations at that time required these civil servants to live within the city limits. Rosedale, on the Queens-Nassau County border, was the furthest into the suburbs they could live. The Club House was the local tavern frequented by many of these men; beer was $.10 a glass (after buying three the bartender usually bought back) and containers could be purchased to take out. Shuffleboard tables were in all the bars (no charge) and as we got older it became the next best thing to basketball. Also, we started thinking more and more about driving and drinking (not necessarily at the same time) but both of which had legal minimum ages of 18. That brings to mind another little story.

The legal drinking age of 18 was enforced at most, but not all bars. I always looked young for my age but starting at about 16, I could get served at Mulvaney's bar in Laurelton, only a short walk from Rosedale. On Friday night a gang of us would go there, drink beer and play shuffleboard until three or four o'clock in the morning and then stagger home. It was the first time I experienced spinning bedrooms and terrible hangovers.

At 18, I received my draft card (World War II was only five years in the past and there was still a draft), which was the standard ID for being served alcoholic beverages. This opened up an entire new world for me; I could now legally buy a drink in any bar (my goals in life were not exceptionally high at the time).

I was now old enough to get a New York State driver's license. However, I had a problem; my left eye's vision was too poor to pass the required eye exam. My friend Billy Quill, had good eyes but had a different problem - he was 17, looked it, and his beer drinking was therefore limited to places like Mulvaney's. What to do? Well we put our two heads (and three eyes) together and made a deal. Billy would go to the Motor Vehicle Bureau with my identification (draft card) fill out the forms, take the eye test, sign my name and return with a learner's permit in my name (no photo ID then). My job was a little easier and required less deviousness – just go to the Selective Service (draft) Board, tell them I lost my draft card, get another one and give it to Billy.

It was a perfect scheme and it worked perfectly except for one embarrassing incident. We both went into a bar together one night where we were proofed by a bartender, who really did not believe we were twin brothers with identical names - and threw us out. There are times when crime does not pay.

The Brookville Park boat caper

My "cousin" Jimmy and I got up shortly after sunrise and went to George Bobka's home where we awakened him by pulling on the string hanging out his window. The other end was tied to his big toe. He quickly dressed and tip toed out of his house as we began our little boat caper. On the way to the lake in Brookville Park we shared with George the milk we had taken from in front of the supermarket.

At the lake one of the rowboats had "accidently" been left unlocked by our fellow conspirator, Walter Clarke. We paddled it to the far end, then managed to drag it across 147th Avenue to the swamps where we planned to hide it. Pushing it through the creeks surrounded by high reeds we felt safe, until we reached an open area where we were confronted by a tough looking, bearded man standing there with a shotgun. It was John August, who lived with his family in a broken down old shack out there in the swamps. His kids had names like Franklin Delano August, Cordel Hull August and other well-known people of the time. In addition to his many children, he ran a decrepit riding academy. I didn't think he had a phone but he did manage to call the police.

Our rock solid alibi - that we just found the boat - was not corroborated by my 10-year-old stepbrother who yelled out the window when the police brought us home, "I see they caught you stealing the boat". However although nothing ever happened to George, Jimmy or me, Walter lost his job at the boathouse and instead of being paid, he had to pay the boat concessionaire $17 for all the candy he had eaten.

The V-12 Lincoln Zephyr

Mattie Fay bought it off the lot for $50 (a few friends had to chip in to make the purchase, there were no insurance requirements in those days and gas was $.30 a gallon). I was with him the night he tried to teach Theresa Martin to drive

We were near Rosedale Station and across from an open-air fruit stand. Terry kept stalling the car when trying to get started, as it required some coordination to manually shift into first gear while slowly depressing the gas pedal and gradually releasing the clutch. (There were no automatic transmissions at the time.) Mattie kept saying, "Give it more gas, Terry. Give it more gas". And that she did!

That gigantic twelve cylinder tank shot across the street, crashed headlong into the ram shackle old fruit stand and carried it into the middle of the next street. We removed the fractured structure from the car and Mattie drove home. Theresa did not learn to drive that night.

It is just one of the many tales of growing up in Rosedale.

YOU'RE IN THE ARMY NOW

Paratroopers Boarding a C-47

I went into the U.S. Army an aimless kid and came out a grown up (sort of).

I was going to be 19 years old in a few months. After four and a half years commuting from Rosedale, Queens to Brooklyn Tech, I still had not graduated from high school. It was an hour and a half commute each way. A five cents bus ride from the next to last stop on the Q5A in Rosedale to the very last stop in Jamaica, where the New York City subway had its most eastbound stop at 169th Street. From there for another nickel I took the F train to Queens Plaza (20 minutes standing room only) and then transferred to the GG local where I was wedged into another sardine can for the 20 minute ride to Fulton Street.

It was February 1951, I had failed a number of courses over the years and still needed one more semester of English along with the Regents to get my diploma. I did not really care. School would not be in my thoughts for the next few years.

Signing up

At the time, the Korean War was being fought and the draft was in effect. I had tried for a couple of jobs but no one was interested in hiring someone without a high school diploma and who would likely be soon drafted. Walter Tinney and I decided to join up. I vaguely remember going into Manhattan for my physical and then for some reason did not leave with Walter. I was sent to Fort Devens, Massachusetts for indoctrination, and then shipped by train to Fort Leonard Wood, Missouri. The first few days I was homesick, not for my dysfunctional home, but for my friends. I was also lonely, surrounded by strangers and living in this totally controlled environment. (I had lived the last five years with no restrictions on what hours I kept or what I did or did not do. Don't get me wrong, I did not do anything especially bad, but did not do anything good either. That was why after four and a half years in high school I still had not graduated.) However, the loneliness quickly passed and I became friends with a few young recruits and pretty much got along with everybody else. However, the strict discipline remained difficult for me to take and in general I disliked being in the service.

We were told when to get up, when to go to bed, what clothes to wear, how to wear them. We were told what to do and where to do it. It was the most boring, tedious, non-productive period of my life. Looking back, it was most likely one of the best things that ever happened to me. I went in a wise-guy kid who had no idea where he was going in life and came out a person whose head was screwed on a little bit tighter. I really don't know what lessons I learned – maybe it was just growing three years older – but the U. S. Army took good care of me during that time. They provided a disciplined life style with three meals each day and a place to sleep each night. They never sent me to Korea and the only fighting I did was in a couple of fistfights. But let me tell you what I remember of the details of that time period fifty years after the fact.

Basic Training

At Fort Leonard Wood I first became acquainted with the domicile I would be living in for the next three years – army barracks. I live such a private life right now it is hard to imagine life in those barracks. Forty soldiers in one room. Ten double bunks on either side of a center aisle with a small shelf behind each bunk and a short clothing bar that held a few hangars. Most clothes and other possessions were contained in footlockers at the foot of the bunks. A separate room at the end of the barracks contained the latrine. It had six freestanding toilets side-by-side, with one having a label above it stating VD Seat (anyone with VD would certainly never use it), a single trough urinal, a few sinks and a shower room with four or five showerheads. Coal furnaces heated the barracks with an assigned company fireman responsible for banking the fire late at night and adding coal and stoking the fire about 5 AM each morning. Friday night we had G.I. parties. Such a euphemism. Hours were spent preparing for the Saturday morning inspection. Floors scrubbed, every surface dusted, latrine spotlessly cleaned – then footlockers were organized in a prescribed way and boots polished. The sergeants inspecting the next morning would invariably find a speck of dust somewhere and the platoon would be gigged. Too many gigs and the Saturday night pass might be revoked or some other punishment imposed.

During the eight weeks of infantry basic training we learned to march (forward march, to the rear march, column left march, to the right flank march); how to fire, clean and fieldstrip our M-1 rifles; fire .30 caliber machine guns and Browning Automatic Rifles (BARs); and throw hand grenades. More than anything we learned discipline, which is necessary if you are going to send young men into battle. But, it was not to my liking.

The next eight weeks I was assigned to engineering basic training. This was more interesting as we learned to use explosives like C-3 and how to build temporary Bailey Bridges. But there were still the weekly G.I. parties and the constant stream of orders being yelled at us all day. Each morning we would line up across the grounds outside the barracks and have police call. "All I want to see is ass-holes and elbows", was bellowed as we crossed the grounds picking up the minutest pieces of foreign material. Cigarette butts were field stripped (there were no filters those days and the paper would be ripped open and tobacco scattered). Almost everyone smoked. Cigarettes were good for you and were cheap. Athletes endorsed them and Arthur Godfrey, a well-known radio personality, promoted them until his cancerous lung had to be removed. We were even given complimentary packs, and the regular ten-minute breaks each hour during the day were the perfect time to light up.

Sometime during this period I volunteered to join the paratroopers. This was my chance to be a hero. So far the army was not what I expected – it was worse than high school. Maybe it would change now. It did not.

After basic training I was given a short leave before reporting to the Infantry School at Fort Benning, Georgia. I managed to hitch a ride on an Air Force plane going to New York. It was the first time I had been in an airplane. It would be the only time I landed in one for many years, even though I took off twenty five times.

Airborne Training

I reported to Fort Benning in mid-July 1951 for three weeks of jump school. It is two weeks of preparation and then a week of jumping. There is a fair amount of calisthenics, running and other physical conditioning, but everyone was young, healthy and in good condition to begin with. (After all we had just finished sixteen weeks of basic training where we did not have the chance to dissipate ourselves.) However, some of the specific training for the jumps was interesting.

PLFs

Parachute landing falls were the first things we learned and we practiced them each day. It is very simple. Just jump from a platform about table height, into a sand pit. The technique is to take up most of the impact in your legs and then roll such that the fleshy parts of the body absorb the rest of the shock. Feet, thighs, buttocks and back of shoulders. We would do this over and over again, jumping off forward, to either side and backwards – simulating the various ways we might be meeting the earth, only in two weeks we would be landing quite a bit harder. (While others were going to college I was learning how to fall. But it was not a total waste. The ability to perform PLFs has helped me survive many falls while skiing and a few years ago I performed a splendid PLF when I fell off the clothes drier while trying to fix a shelf).

Suspended Harness

Although the real name of this contraption was the suspended harness it was referred to colloquially as the nutcracker or ball breaker. It was a parachute harness suspended a couple of feet off the ground. We would get into it, connect the quick release buckles and hang there while given instructions on how to control the direction of the chute (pull down on the two risers – there are four – in the direction you want to go) and then hope to avoid the other trooper you are about to entangle, or miss the tree you are heading for.

Wind Machine

Sometimes the wind blows quite hard when landing and we were shown how to avoid being dragged across the Drop Zone (DZ). A parachute on the ground with one of the cadre in the harness was set in the path of air blown from a 15-foot fan. The chute billowed out and started to drag the instructor. However, he rolled around, got his feet pointing towards the parachute so that it pulled him to his feet, then ran around to the downwind side of the chute and collapsed it. It worked for the instructor, but some time later while landing in a high wind I was dragged what seemed halfway across Texas (that is where our maneuvers were) before someone else jumped on my chute. I in turn helped another trooper by doing the same thing. So much for theory.

The 34 Foot Tower

If there is anything I remember about jump school it is the 34-foot tower. Not many people failed out of jump school (there were no Regents) but for the few that did, it was the result of the 34-foot tower. We would climb the tower stairs in single file wearing a parachute harness (no parachute, just the harness with a simulated reserve chute) until we reached the mock-up aircraft exit door. From there we attached our harness to a ten-foot heavy-duty simulated parachute riser that had its other end attached to a pulley that rode on an overhead cable that gradually sloped to the ground. The idea was to learn to exit an airplane using the proper technique.

An instructor on the ground would give the signal to jump and we would do just that, with our heads down, arms across the reserve chute (to be used in actual jumps if the main chute malfunctioned) and shouting, "one thousand, two thousand, three thousand". When done properly we would reach the end of the riser while saying "three thousand" and swallow the last couple of syllables as our fall was jerked to a sudden stop. This simulated the real chute as it popped open (if it did not open for an actual jump, the D handle on the reserve chute was pulled). From there it was a short ride down the cable where a couple of G.I.'s would unhook us from the riser and we would go back up and do it again. The ground instructor would also critique our exit technique. Sounds easy, and it was physically, but the idea of looking way down to that tiny instructor on the ground, so far away, and waiting for him to yell, "jump", terrified many. A few trainees would get so nervous they couldn't concentrate on the proper way to make the tower jump and eventually washed out. I was not terrified – just scared the first couple of times. It was the thought of jumping out of an airplane flying at 1000 feet that was starting to get to me.

There was a story that a member of a certain minority, that many of the southern boys believed to be of inferior mentality, forgot to hook up properly, and when making the tower jump went crashing directly to the ground. As he slowly picked himself up from the dirt he said, "If it gets any rougher than this, I quit".

The 250-Foot Tower

The 250-foot towers were the last pieces of equipment used in preparation for the five jumps we would make in our third and last week of jump school. Real parachutes, with us hanging from them, were hauled up 250 feet and then released for our first real parachute jump experience. Risers were pulled to control direction and then about 50 feet above the ground we would look out to the horizon (not at the ground) and prepare for the landing. Legs slightly bent, hands high on the risers, aware of the direction we were traveling so that we could execute the correct PLF. *Lots of luck.* But we did remember some of it and after a few tries we were getting the hang of it. Although much higher than the 34-foot tower it was nowhere near as frightening. Don't know why.

On Friday we finished our second week of training and Monday would be the real thing. Most of the guys (there were only guys at the time in the Army) had never been in an airplane before. It would be interesting. Personally, I was getting more and more nervous – and I had been in a plane once. I was not sure I would be able to go through with it and was asking others who already had their wings just what it was like. Their assurances did not help very much and I spent an anxious weekend going over and over in my mind the feeling I would have when I stepped to the aircraft door, was tapped on the butt and told, "Jump".

Jumps – the real thing

Week three of training came, and on Monday morning we were taken by bus to Lawson Field an air base within Fort Benning. We lined up for our main and reserve parachutes, then waited for what seemed like hours until told to board our C-47 airplanes (these were the military versions of the Douglas DC-3). There were 28 of us in each plane, sitting on two benches running along either side of the fuselage. Lee Field, also within the Fort Benning confines, was the drop zone (DZ) and the flight to it lasted only a few minutes. As we approached, a red light by the door flashed and the jumpmaster, who was standing near the two open doors, gave us the following commands:

"Standup"

"Hook up" - We attached our static lines to a head high cable running the length of the plane. The other end of the static line was attached to the parachute backpack and pulled open the chute shortly after we exited the plane

"Check equipment" - We checked our own equipment and the chute on the back of the G.I. next to us

"Sound off for equipment check" - We sounded off in sequence that the equipment checked out OK

"Shuffle and stand in the door" - The first troopers in each stick (that is what the line of troopers on each side of the plane were called) shuffled into the open doors holding either side of the doorframe. Everyone else moved up as close as possible to the person in front of them.

"Jump" - This command was given when the green light was activated by the pilot. It was followed by a tap on the rear-end by the jumpmaster and the two sticks of parachutists then exited the aircraft in a matter of seconds.

I was scared silly and the main reason I remember this is that it was noted in my jump log, where I recorded my first ten jumps. But I did jump, and I did it again and again over the next two and a half years for a total of 25 jumps. As time went on, I would still be nervous while shuffling toward that open door, but did not have any serious anxieties prior to the actual jump.

That third and final week of jump school, we made single jumps on Monday and Tuesday, two jumps on Wednesday and one on Thursday. Friday was graduation and we received our paratrooper wings that I eventually lost (as I do many things). However, I did buy another set in the PX, did not lose them, and eventually gave them to Barbara who attached them to her charm bracelet.

508th Airborne Regimental Combat Team

After completing jump school I was assigned to the 508th Airborne Regimental Combat Team. It had been part of the famous 82nd Airborne Division that participated in a number of combat jumps in WWII, and at the time I wore the AA patch (it stood for All American as all 48 states were represented in it). The 508th was deactivated shortly after WWII and then reactivated in 1951 with its own distinctive patch. We also wore a patch on our fatigues showing a red devil coming down in a parachute. We were naturally called the Red Devils. The Red Devils would be my home at Fort Benning for the next two and a half years.

What did I do during that time? The answer – go through basic training over and over again. Get up early and run.

Hup, two, three four,
hup, two, three, four,
you had a good home but you left
your right - sound off,
one, two, three, four,
one, two - three four.

March for miles with full field packs and weapons, and be subject to inspections, inspections, inspections. Not just the barracks. We had to get haircuts just about every week. Our daily work clothes – our fatigues – were washed and starched by the company laundry (at our expense). Some of my fellow troopers would go crazy spit shining their paratrooper boots that were seldom worn because then they would lose their shine.

Our infantry company would regularly go to the rifle range where we would shoot at and also work the targets (pulling targets up for the shooters, then pulling them down for scoring and patching up the holes). When firing was completed and if a target was missed completely, the GI working the target would wave a red flag and this was called "Maggie's Drawers".

(In retrospect this was not so bad. Other trainees were being sent to Korea as replacement troops and getting themselves killed and maimed.)

Someone read about another airborne company having a dog that jumped with them. Sounded like a great idea, so we took up a collection and for a hundred dollars bought a German shepherd puppy we named Devil. That ferocious sounding name was considered appropriate, as we were the Red Devils. A more appropriate name for this cowardly canine would have been Shadow. Devil was afraid of everything. Even when full grown, the local mongrel pups would give a yip and send him cowering into the barracks. I remember that frankfurter skins had to be removed before he would eat them. On marches, he would get as far as the end of the company street, then turn tail and head back to his bed. Devil jump? Forget about it!

Base pay for a Private First Class (PFC), which I was for most of the time, was $120 per month. Not much, but there were no living expenses and everything on the base was cheap. Soda was a nickel, movies a quarter and beer sold for a quarter a bottle. We also received an extra $50 a month jump pay, provided we jumped once every three months. I averaged almost one per month, making 20 more jumps after completing airborne training. Some were routine, made with a minimum of extra equipment and were relatively easy. Some were not.

Night jump

This jump was performed without any extra field equipment, but it was a strange feeling stepping out into the black void of space. Once the chute opened, I just hung there totally disoriented until the earth suddenly whacked me successively on the soles of my feet, thigh, behind and shoulder as I did a perfect (?) PLF.

Equipment jumps

On one jump I carried a .30 caliber air-cooled machine gun that weighed about 50 pounds. It was in a padded container hooked onto two D-rings of my parachute harness. Also carried was my field pack, shelter half (it is half a tent that you combine with a buddy to make a tent), sleeping bag, canteen, ammunition, entrenching tool, C-rations and whatever other equipment needed for a few days of living and conducting maneuvers in the field. I figured it was going to be a horrible few days.

But I was wrong.

I was somewhere in the middle of the stick when the command "Shuffle and stand at the door", was given. I could just about stand, but I did manage to stumble, if not shuffle, to the open door and fall out into empty space. The chute opened and everything was going smoothly, except I was going a little faster than usual and hit the ground hard. I guess it was a less than perfect PLF. The net result was a million dollar injury. In combat that is an injury that will completely heal but gets a G.I. back home – for me it was a bruised rear-end that would get me back to the barracks and not have to play soldier out in the field for the next three days.

On another tactical full equipment jump, the wind was extremely high and I landed hard on my rifle before being dragged halfway across the DZ. I was not hurt this time but it did put a noticeable bend in my rifle. Also some canned food in my lower leg pockets was badly mashed.

Tree jump

One of our non-equipment or training jumps was a disaster as the jumpmaster was nervous and did not signal the stick of troopers to jump until a few seconds after the green light started to flash. It does not take long for an airplane to traverse the DZ and the last few troopers in the stick ended up in the trees. There were quite a few injuries as a result.

Social condition

I should briefly mention something about social conditions in the South. In New York where I had lived all my life segregation existed, and still does, but was not sanctioned by law. I never associated with many blacks, but ate in restaurants with them, sat or stood with them on buses and subways and went to all sorts of public events where they also attended with no special seating arrangements. In my naïve way of life I never thought much about blacks. I did know that my stepmother referred to Jews as "kikes" and Italians as "Guineas", but not too much about blacks that were called colored people in polite

35

circles (years later I would hear Barbara's mother refer to black women as "negresses"). However, on one of my first trips to the nearby city of Columbus, Georgia I noticed a sign outside a gas station – colored water. I wondered if it was a Kool-Aid type of drink. I soon found out. Although the army had been recently integrated (there were a few blacks in basic training) this was my first "Southern Experience".

However, the experience that sticks in my mind after all these years, happened on one of my trips traveling back from leave in New York to Georgia. My mode of travel was always hitchhiking and it would usually take me about a day and a half to make the 800-mile trip. (A number of times I would be stuck on some lonely road in the middle of the night waiting for a ride.) On this particular journey I was picked up by a black man someplace in New Jersey (there was no Jersey Turnpike at the time – in fact there were very few Interstate Highways of any kind) and driving through Maryland we stopped for some coffee and a snack. I started to go through the main entrance, but stopped when he said he had to go to the rear entrance – the one for colored people. I was embarrassed. Here was this nice man, who had gone out of his way to pick up a young kid in a soldier's suit, being treated as a second-class citizen. And this happened to him every day. I was no longer reading about segregation, I was seeing and being a part of it.

The fight

I guess I insulted Jimmy Gagnon (the company cook – a somewhat overweight, out of conditioned ex-boxer) one night while in Phoenix City, Alabama. This was just across the river from Columbus and was considered Sin City because of all the bars, strip joints, and loose women (some even had tattoos). I don't remember the details except he said something about getting me when we got back to the base. I paid no attention until the next day when Jimmy came up to me and said, "Let's go into that empty barracks and settle this". I still to this day do not know his reason, but being a young testosterone engorged, "lean, mean, fighting machine" replied, "Yeah".

A short time later Jimmy left the barracks covered with blood. At first glance everyone thought he had been thoroughly beaten – Domjan must be quite a fighter. Slight mistake. The blood was mine and when my battered and bruised body emerged shortly after, the next stop was the battalion medic where a nervous corpsman put three stitches in my lip. So much for this lean, mean, fighting machine.

Bridge jump

The bridge over the Chattahoochee River that connects Phoenix City and Columbus is about 40 feet above the water. One night, after one too many, Wes (I forget his last name) in a kidding way said, "I'll bet $5 you won't dive off the bridge". Without giving it a second thought, over the bridge railing I went, headfirst into the disgustingly cruddy water (luckily there was sufficient water). Some women working in a riverside mill saw the event and started screaming "Suicide". I instantly sobered up as I swam to shore and scrambled back to meet my friends, thinking of the consequences facing me back at camp if caught. For the next few days I got these strange looks from G.I.'s in the mess hall as they whispered, "There's the guy that jumped off the bridge".

Field Wireman School

I had been in the army for about 18 months (half way through) and had risen to the grand rank of corporal. While those at home may have completed three college semesters and others in the service were developing skills in electronics or other trades, all I had learned was how to fall on my ass without breaking it.

So I felt great joy and anticipation when told I would be going to Field Wireman Training in Fort Jackson, South Carolina. This would be great. It was not. The only interesting thing I can remember was climbing the 30-foot utility poles. We strapped steel gaffs (spikes) onto our legs, leaned out as far as possible while still holding onto the pole and then climbed. There is a tendency to not want to lean out, but if you don't, the gaffs won't stay jammed into the wooden pole and you slide down accumulating numerous gigantic splinters along the length of your body.   I survived, but it was always entertaining watching other students occasionally bite the dust.

However, the classroom instructions were interminably boring and I started to go to the base library instead. The magazines were a lot more interesting – until I got caught. I was hauled before the company commander and was busted on the spot. PFC Domjan went back to the dull classes, completed training and returned to Fort Benning, somewhat embarrassed by his demotion.

Locked in

In 1953 I was 21 years old (looked considerably younger), five feet seven and 135 pounds. I looked sharp in my uniforms (either pressed and starched fatigues or Class A) and spit-shined paratrooper boots, but certainly did not look the part of the Military Policeman that my armband indicated. You might ask just what was I doing in the MPs? Looking back I might ask the same question.

It seems there was a shortage of MPs and some of the 508th troops were "volunteered" for temporary duty as Military Policemen. Most of my time was spent at the main gate waving in vehicles with the proper authorization plates. It was boring and to relieve the tedium we would occasionally go on "by the rule book" crusades, stopping vehicles with minor infractions like burned out taillights and giving citations. This was fun since we were lowly enlisted men and the offenders were often lieutenants, captains and above.

Sometimes, but not too often I would be assigned duty in Columbus, or Phoenix City. I would parade through town, with my imposing presence striking fear into any soldier contemplating a misdeed. Yeah! Actually not much happened while on duty in town and all I remember is checking ages of some G.I.s in a few of the clubs. Off-duty was another story.

One night while sitting alone in a Columbus bar I realized that I was really alone. No other customers, no waiters, no manager, no bartenders. Shortly before that I had gone to the men's room, stayed a little longer than usual and then returned to my barstool. The jukebox was still playing, my drink was on the bar and although a little darker, the place was still lit. I figured the young barmaids were in the back room doing something and I continued to drink my beer and listen to the music till it eventually ended. It was then I realized I was really alone. (The barmaids, anxious to do the town themselves before everything closed, had hastily left and locked the joint while I was in the bathroom.) It was now time for me to leave, but there was one problem – the front door was locked.

Having an analytical mind (I did become an engineer) I looked at and analyzed various solutions. I could break the window (stupid), stay in the bar and drink myself to oblivion (the choice of many fellow troopers when they later heard of my misadventure) or call for help (the logical choice). Luckily I had a single dime and also knew the phone number of the MP station in Columbus (there was no such thing as 911). I called and told the desk sergeant, who I knew, of my plight. He thought I was kidding and it was only my desperate voice that convinced him I was truly locked in a bar in downtown Columbus, Georgia. MPs arrived a few minutes later and we waved back and forth through the windows of the bar. Luckily the owner's number was on the front door (why didn't I see it?) whom they called. The rescue was completed shortly after and everybody, except the proprietor, had a good belly laugh.

Prison Chaser

A horrible detail that would come up occasionally was "prison chaser". This entailed getting up at 4:30 AM and taking a truck ride to Fort Benning's main post where we received a one-hour indoctrination on the responsibilities of taking prisoners from the army stockade out on daily work details. No matter how many times we had received prison chaser duties the indoctrination was always the same – long and boring. (The unofficial word was that if a prisoner escaped you had to complete his sentence. And it was always a his, there were no hers at the time.)

The job I remember was garbage collection. Standing in the back of an open truck, knee deep in garbage and holding my trusty shotgun, the two or three prisoners assigned to me would perform their task as we made the rounds of the company refuse sites. It should be noted that based on my KP experience (another horrible duty) garbage was separated into garbage pails labeled ashes (we used coal stoves), glass, tin cans, edible and non-edible. Just like today's recycling - except all the garbage was dumped into one truck.

The day was spent with these prisoners, who if they were real desperados, could have thrown a pail of garbage on me, taken my shotgun, stolen the truck and still be living with some local militia group. Luckily for me they were just ordinary guys, thrown in the jug for a month or two for being AWOL, drunk or committing some other relatively minor infraction.

Discharge

Sometime before my discharge in February 1954, I was promoted back to Corporal. Also, I took a United States Armed Forces Institute (USAFI) correspondence course that allowed me to take the New York State English regents. On leave in January 1954 I went to Brooklyn Tech, took the test and passed with a magnificent 66. I was awarded my high school diploma just seven and a half year after starting high school, and was now a bona fide graduate. With my honorable discharge, high school diploma and outstanding ability to perform PLFs, I was ready to take on the world.

to fly

There is a wide screen IMAX film titled TO FLY. It has spectacular aerial shots of all sorts of flying machines that can make you dizzy. My own personal non-spectacular story of aviation is appropriately kept to lower case letters.

For as long as I can remember I have been interested in flying. Not fanatical, like the Wright brothers or all those early pioneers, or like those who became astronauts, not even like those interested enough to actually learn to fly. But more like a boyhood fascination with airplanes as they flew overhead, who loved to build balsa wood model planes, not for display but to fly (actually most of them were contemporary WWII fighter planes that as scale models did not fly well with their rubber band engines). However, interested enough to jump off the garage roof with a sheet as a parachute (successful in that I did not break a leg, unsuccessful with respect to slowing my rate of descent). Interested enough to take the aero course in high school and then get my Bachelor of Aeronautical Engineering Degree from Brooklyn Polytech.

My first real opportunity to fly was as a paratrooper in the U.S. Army where I made 25 jumps, each one of about a minute's duration (not much accumulated flight time).

After the service I went to Brooklyn Polytech where I majored in Aeronautical Engineering (see endnote). My first job was to be with Republic Aviation, but I lost that when I failed two subjects in my senior year and did not graduate. I received my degree a year later, but by then was employed by the Sperry Gyroscope Company where for the next few years I worked on of all things – submarines. How low could I go!

During this period, one of my interests was in the building and flying of a man-carrying water skiing kite - a huge contraption of wood and canvas. That is a separate story in itself and is the subject of the following assay, "The Kite".

However, my professional aviation career took a turn for the better when I left the Sperry submarines and went to work for Grumman on the Apollo Program. Grumman built the Lunar Modules that landed on the moon in 1969 and I worked on their navigation and guidance systems. I even had the opportunity to work on one of the LMs being assembled in a dust free clean room. But I was not flying.

Hang gliding

After the moon landing in 1969 the space program was severely cut back and so was I. I lost my job with Grumman and went back to Sperry, but this time as a traffic engineer. One of the jobs took me to Norfolk, Virginia, which is only a couple of hours from the Outer Banks in North Carolina (the state with "First in Flight" on its license plates). The Wright Brothers came to Kitty Hawk on the Outer Banks because of the sand dunes and steady winds that allowed them to experiment with gliders and then powered aircraft. Eighty years later it was those same sand dunes and steady winds that brought Kitty Hawk Kites to the Outer Banks to open up their hang gliding school. It would be another chance for me "to fly".

After a one-hour classroom lesson, I was atop a hundred foot dune, strapped to a fifty-pound hang-glider and attempting to fly. I started jogging down the hill, pushed out the control bar and took off. By God, I was flying, but only for a short time - as I had pushed the control bar out too far, stalled the glider and crashed. It was typical of most flights that day, which were short (on the order of a few seconds) and ended in crashes. No one was ever hurt as the flights were slow and the sand soft enough to go barefoot. It was fun, but it was hot and it was hard work carrying the glider back up the hill for the next flight. I went back for lessons on two other occasions but never got any better. It was nothing like what you see in the movies – we never were more than about ten feet off the ground, if that much. It was definitely a lower case version of "to fly".

Flying lessons

Although fascinated by flight, the thought of flying a plane never entered my mind; I was essentially blind in one eye. Wiley Post flew with a patch over his blind eye but that was in the early days of flight when there was no Federal Aviation Administration (FAA) with its multitude of rules and regulations governing flying. And besides, with one eye, three-dimensional vision was not possible. Catching or hitting a baseball had always been difficult for me and tennis balls would seem to go "through" my racket (larger objects like footballs and basketballs were no problem).

Then one day, while working on a traffic job in Virginia (it was about 1980) one of the electrical subcontractors mentioned he would be taking flying lessons even though he was blind in one eye – said the regulations allowed it. I mentally filed that little remark away for future reference.

By 1993, with the mortgage paid, the kids on their own and a few dollars in the bank, I decided to check on flying lessons. At Mid Island Air Service (located at MacArthur Airport, just five minutes from my office) I inquired about flying lessons for a half blind, late middle (early old) age man. No problem. FAA regulations allowed it and there were many pilots with that condition (maybe that is why there are so many plane crashes - I know that I was not sure of my ability to judge height when landing). Lessons started that fall, and I learned to take-off, recover from stalls and perform other maneuvers. However, I never got to landings as I developed a little problem with my arteries. Seems they were blocked and required bypass surgery.

The operation was a success but the patient did not think so and I went for some more tests that were inconclusive. As a result, I did not get a completely clean bill of health, and when I tried to get reinstated for flying, the FAA said "no dice" you are not healthy. Discouraged, but not completely beaten I turned to gliding.

At Gabreski Airport in Westhampton Beach there is a glider school that I visited and asked about requirements. They told me that for unpowered flight, physicals are not necessary. I went to the FAA office at Republic Airport in Farmingdale and received my Airman Certificate, good for learning to fly balloons and gliders. Back at Gabreski I went for a few lessons. However, they were expensive, only lasted a few minutes and did not seem very cost effective. Gliding was not for me. However, they were interesting, being slowly towed to an altitude of a thousand feet, releasing the towline, and then soaring silently above the airport and surrounding countryside. The gliders or sailplanes as they are called are very ruggedly built and can be flown aerobatically. (Not like the Cessnas I had been taking powered flight lessons in - they had to be carefully flown within restrictive limits.) During one lesson, the instructor put the glider into a spin and scared the hell out of me. He then wanted to show me how it could loop, but I said, "No thanks".

I then wrote the FAA. Told them how healthy I was and asked to be reinstated. Surprisingly they did, although I had to take cardiac stress tests each year along with the normal biannual physical. Lessons started again along with home study of a $500 computer program on basic flying theory and the FAA regulations required to pass their written test. I was progressing slowly and methodically (even made a few bumpy landings) but noticed it was getting more difficult to adjust my eyes to the instrument panel and to clearly observe nearby aircraft that my instructor always saw. When it came time to renew my physical, there were some problems that required a further explanation from my doctor. I probably could have gotten it, but decided it might be a good time to just pack it in. And I did.

The cycle has now been completed. In 2003 I built a balsa wood model of the Wright Flyer, the heavier-than-air machine that made the first powered flight just one hundred years earlier in 1903. Flying and aviation are still not out of my system.

End Note: 50th College Reunion

Although scheduled to graduate from Brooklyn Polytech in 1958 with a Bachelor's degree in Aeronautical Engineering, I stumbled a bit and got the degree a year later. However, when the class of '58 celebrated its 50th anniversary, my good friend Don MacKenzie whom I first met at Poly got me invited. In those five decades I had not been in contact with any of my classmates except for Don and did not realize the extent of their distinguished careers until I read their biographies. They were heavily laden with expressions like; Supervisor of Aerothermochemistry and Viscous Flow, Expert Assistant to Nuclear Reactor Safety Division, Project Engineer on Minuteman Re-entry System's Penetration Aids Program, Director of Engineering and Research, Executive Director of the U.S. Secretariat for International Global Observing of Systems Programs. And this is just a sampling. It is hard to imagine what the world would have become without the accomplishments of my distinguished fellow alumni. So it was with great trepidation that I began to review my own career and prepare a short talk for the reunion in May 2008.

I knew I could not compete on the same playing field with any of my fellow grads. In the 49 years since receiving my belated degree I had worked on submarine navigation systems, lunar space ships and roadway traffic systems – never on anything that flew through the air. But really, how many of them had attempted to hang glide or learn to fly an airplane instead of designing one? The one thing I was certain they had never tried was to fly a man-carrying kite. So that was what I talked about along with showing an 8 x 10 glossy of me and my kite. It was very low tech compared with what my compatriots achieved and yet I thought it went over well. Not everyone agreed. Jackie MacKenzie, Don's wife, thought it was dumb and my wife said I embarrassed her. A stumble? Maybe.

THE KITE

"Then I saw the kite"

Me and kite in 1959

As part of my interest in flying, the kite story deserves a special essay of its own.

It was around 1955 that I first got interested in water-skiing. For the past few years articles about water skiing at Cypress Gardens, Florida had appeared in popular publications such as Life and Look magazines and I was fascinated by them. At that time there was some limited water skiing going on in the Long Island waters, and although a few of my friends had boats, none had skis. Water skis were expensive and nobody was very interested....except me and I had no extra cash (I had just started attending Hofstra College). However, as fate would have it, I came across an article in Popular Mechanics Magazine on how to build water skis. It seemed so simple reading the step-by-step instructions. The skis would practically build themselves.

Building water skis

At the time I was living in the Tulip Hill Bowling Lanes in Floral Park while attending college (but that's another story – see "School Days").

The Popular Mechanics do-it-yourself instructions required two - 6 foot 1 x 8's for the basic skis, a sheet of Bakelite or similar plastic for attaching the bindings to the skis, and some heavy rubber sheeting for the bindings themselves. Templates were included for layouts of the bindings and attachments. The lumberyard provided the wood, an old inner tube from a car tire provided the rubber (in those days car tires had tubes) and I found some pieces of scrap plastic. Also required was some scrap lumber to construct a form for bending the tips of the wooden planks into the shape of water skis. After building the form, the instructions said to steam the wood until it became bendable and then clamp it to the form until it permanently retained the correct shape. I did not have access to any steaming equipment, but working in the bowling alley allowed me to use the kitchen - I ate the blue plate special there almost every night – where I planned to "boil, not steam my wood". (The hamburger and French fry special would eventually lead to major artery problems years later, but that is also another story.)

To the consternation, but grudging approval of the bowling alley owners, I was allowed to use a twenty-gallon soup pot to "prepare" my wooden planks for the bending operation. In the kitchen, along with the greasy burgers and fries, I stuck the six-foot boards into the pot of boiling water. They stayed in that pot for the better part of a day as I regularly checked them for any sign of softening that would make the bending operation easier and more effective. However, they just got hot and wet... and remained stiff.

Eventually I was told, "Enough is enough, get that crap out of the kitchen".

The next step was to bend my boiled boards around the homemade form that was in the bowling alley basement next to the beer kegs. This proved to be more difficult than expected as the wood had not softened very much and resisted changing shape. (Years later I found out that horizontal saw cuts in the ski tips allowed for easier bending.) Eventually I did get the wood to bend to the form using heavy duty C-clamps and much muscle power. They were then left to "cure".

After a week I tried loosening the clamps but the skis started to return to their original God–given shape and the clamps had to be re-tightened. I waited another week. The same thing happened again, and I waited again. This occurred a number of times until I finally realized the skis were in their final shape; they weren't going to bend no more, no more. Although they did not have the curvature I had planned on – they were more like snow skis – they did appear functional.

Now for the bindings. The rubber inner tube and plastic were cut to shape and attached to the skis. The only problem was that commercial bindings used molded rubber, shaped to stand up for easy foot insertion. Mine were flat rubber that wanted to stay flat after being attached to the skis. The result was a two-dimensional ski with a two-dimensional binding; they were not only difficult to get into, but once on, difficult to get the flat ski tips out of the water to get started. Imagine treading water (we did not use life jackets at the time), holding a tow line, trying to jam on an ill-fitting water ski while hoping the other ski doesn't drift away, and eventually yelling "hit it" to the boat skipper, while trying to keep the skis properly aligned and tips above the surface. But if you struggled enough they worked and we were actually able to ski and had an entertaining time using them. (I later discovered that some people skied on bare feet and skiing on homemade skis was really no big deal.)

Then I saw the kite.

It was a picture – again from Cypress Gardens – of a water skier suspended about 100 feet in the air by a huge kite, the same shape as those I flew as a kid, only ten times larger. The water skiing seed implanted in my brain a few years earlier was about to sprout. I spoke to my good friend Bob Rossman and his brother Dick about the possibility of building one of these contraptions. They both said, "Go for it". (They also provided me, who has only one good eye and limited driving ability, with a stock car to race at Freeport Raceway. So much for their good judgment)

This time there was no article from Popular Mechanics on how to build a man-carrying kite, only a small photo of a flying water skier. However, from this, we could roughly guess at the kite's size and proportions; it would be ten feet high and nine feet wide. It would be made from whatever material the Rossmans could provide.

It resulted in the fabric being cut out from an old WW II dayglow pink rubberized canvas life raft, and a frame made from 1 x 2 inch scrap lumber. However, after assembling these components, we ran into a problem – where on the kite should the tow-bar be attached? This bar is tied to the towline pulled by the boat and the airborne skier hangs by his arms directly below it. If attached too far forward the kite will angle down too much and won't provide sufficient lift to fly, too far back and the kite will be too vertical to fly.

What to do? The answer? – experimental land based flight-testing (after all I was now almost a genuine bonafide graduate aeronautical engineer). With a bar temporarily in position about three feet below the kite center, a towline was attached to it and propulsion provide by three fleet footed assistants running down the middle of the road. I was at the other end of the line running with them, holding the tow-bar that was attached to the kite above it. When we reached top speed, I would jump as high as possible and during the brief seconds aloft observers would judge the kite's aerodynamic qualities. Doing this a number of times at different bar positions we were able to determine what appeared to be the best tow-bar location.

Now for the true test.

A number of my friends had boats with sufficient power to pull water skis and we all were able to get up on the skis, jump the wake, ski on one ski and perform other basic "tricks". (By this time many people had store-bought water skis and my "hand crafted" ones had been reduced to kindling.) However, none of this required much more than the power of a 25 horsepower motor on a small boat. With the kite, everything was different. The kite had to be carried on deck, and with its large surface area it was unwieldy and difficult to keep in the boat. Once out in the water-skiing area, the kite and I would be clumsily dropped into the water. Although the kite would float by virtue of its all-wood frame, it did weigh about 40 pounds, which would eventually have to be lifted out of the water to get started. First, I struggled to get the skis on (still no life jacket), then get under the kite which had been tied to the towline, grab the tow bar, and get my ski tips up, all the while hoping the boat operator could maintain some tension in the line without leaving me adrift. Finally I would yell out, in a half-drowned voice, "Hit it". Now normally when the skipper applied full throttle, the water skier - sans kite - would immediately pop out of the water and start skiing. For me, with only my head and a little bit of the kite out of the water, the drag on the boat was so great that it took a while – it seemed like forever - to get sufficient speed to get me and the kite out of the water. During this transition I was struggling to keep my balance while holding up 40 pounds of near dead weight. Needless to say many of these attempts ended in total failures, never getting up on the skis, no less actually flying. On those occasions where I was able to get up and ski with the kite, the boats were never able to pull me fast enough to attain lift-off. There were times when I would jump into the air and stay aloft for a few seconds but there was no sustained flight. In fact for every second in the air there was probably an hour or so of just trying to get out of the water. (But keep in mind the airplane had already been invented and we were having one hell of a good time - with lots of laughs - in our futile attempt to "fly".)

This became part of our summer rituals with a few attempts made each year, but never succeeding because we did not have a boat with enough power. At least that was what we thought the problem was... until the BIG DAY.

It was to be a yak roast with entertainment.

The year was 1962 and the kite had never successfully flown. Although my primary goal in life was not to become a flying water skier, many people knew of my unsuccessful escapades and privately thought of me as one of the Wrong brothers. Personally, I had been having a good time over the past few years, going to the Hamptons on some summer weekends and when not there, occasionally trying to fly my man-carrying kite. This particular summer I had a half-share in a Hampton cottage right on a Peconic Bay sandy beach. This meant that every other weekend I was entitled to stay at this beach house along with a half dozen or so fellow Sperry Gyroscope Company engineers and our friends. After a season of partying, sailing, beaching and in general having a grand old time, we planned a gala "Yak Roast" for the final summer weekend.

This meant digging a pit in the sand, building a fire in it, and then - since yaks were scarce at this time of year - roasting a pig in the heated pit. It also meant providing cases and cases of beer for the many friends we had made all summer and who were invited to join us in our celebration and watch the live entertainment.

The live entertainment was to be a first-time-ever demonstration of the full flight of my man-carrying kite. (It seems that Wally Kuettner, our next door neighbor, had a very powerful speedboat, and he would be more than happy to provide the propulsive force required to take me up into the wild blue yonder.)

Well, the big day arrived and the weather was perfect - bright sunny skies and warm temperature – a great day for an end-of-summer beach party. While the many partygoers were bathing, drinking, and eating roast "yak", I was busy assembling my kite. It required bolting together the frame, rigging the kite fabric to the frame and then attaching the tow-bar. Also, no beer drinking for me, I would not be guilty of FWI (flying while impaired).

Later in the afternoon, with the party in full swing, we decided it was time for the "first flight". This time it would be easier starting since I would be in only chest deep water and would have assistance from some of my friends (although their sobriety was questionable). Offsetting this advantage was the fact that Wally, who was a knowledgeable skipper, did not have any experience pulling man-carrying water ski kites. (For that matter I did not have any experience flying them.) He circled around me trying to get the towline in the proper position, while I struggled to get the water skis on, while holding onto the kite tow-bar, while attempting to get the kite in the proper position behind and slightly over my head. At the same time my friends were trying to tie the towline to the tow-bar while Wally attempted to maintain some tension in the line. (This was an absolute necessity, for if the boat tried to pull me up with a slack line it would result in too much of a jolt for my skinny arms and shoulders.)

On the beach the crowd was getting restive. What was going on? Where was the entertainment? Filled with beer and not appreciating the intricacies of our pre-flight launch preparations, all they saw were a few guys standing about 100 feet offshore, near an inboard speedboat getting ready for what looked like a routine water ski start. Except there was something sticking out of the water behind the skier – something pink.

Then it happened. The confluence of events that started with a chance reading of a Popular Mechanics article on water skis all came together. The building of water skis in a bowling alley kitchen; the construction of a man-carrying kite; the land based flight testing; the years of attempting flights using under-powered boats – all of this was about to culminate in a spectacular demonstration of man's capability to overcome gravity.

Or was it?

I was being steadied on either side by my friends, with my head just barely out of the water, while holding the tow- bar in front of me and with the partially submerged kite resting on my head and back. The skis were on my feet with their tips out of the water and the speedboat was in gear with a throttle setting just high enough to maintain some tension in the towline. Wally was anxiously waiting for the magic words.

When I yelled "Hit it!" – he did. He gave the engine full throttle and it responded with a roar and started to accelerate. (In prior attempts the boats had barely moved because of the drag caused by the kite in the water. Not this time.) In what seemed like a split second I was yanked to the water's surface. Was I about to fly? To soar above the anxious crowd? To vindicate those years of frustrating attempts to break the bonds of gravity?

I had expected to hear the rush of wind lifting the kite and me into the air. I had expected to hear the crowd cheer as I climbed into the sky. Instead, I heard the splintering sound of 1 x 2 frame members once again becoming scrap lumber. I heard my self gasp, "Oh _ _ _ _". I heard the speedboat motor fading into the distance and I heard the crowd groan, "This was the entertainment?"

As I floated in the water surrounded by the wreckage of what used to be my man-carrying kite, I realized we had a new problem - too much power. And not enough brains. I had stumbled again.

I wearily carted the remains of my kite to the beach, threw away what was left of the wooden frame, folded up the day-glow pink rubberized kite fabric - and had a beer.

The kite was never to attempt another flight, and remained a relic of times-gone-by, laying among the accumulated junk in my garage. For this little story, I resurrected it long enough to take a picture and prove to myself that my kite escapade was not just a wild and crazy dream.

Me and kite in 2000

DUKE

It was not the Indianapolis 500, but it was still a thrill.

I am sure you have heard of Duke Ellington and maybe Duke Snyder, but I am just as sure you *never* heard the name "Duke Domjan" even though he drove a stock car at Freeport Municipal Stadium in the late 1950s. He is definitely not in the stock car racing hall of fame. The name is not famous nor will it even go down in infamy. However, one summer evening in 1958 it was clearly heard by a few thousand people at that Freeport Stadium.

"Car 138 has flipped over ladies and gentlemen and the driver aboard is Duke Domjan. We hope he is all right. The ambulance is on its way". A few moments later, "We'll know if he's hurt in just a few seconds – the door is being pried open – Duke is climbing out - and he's giving us the high sign. The Duke is okay folks!"

For the record, the Duke Domjan referenced above is me, although I was never called that by anybody other than the announcers at the raceway. Don't know how the moniker originated, even the name "Bill" was painted on the side of the 1947 Ford sedan I drove at Freeport for a few summers, a long time ago. However, before I continue my story a little description of racing at Freeport is in order.

At some time after the Second World War midget car racing became very popular. These were literally tiny versions of the

55

racecars driven at the Indy 500 and other big car tracks. The tracks the midgets raced at were small – Freeport was a one-quarter mile loop – and speeds topped out at about 60 mph.

Those cars were costly to buy, and expensive to maintain and run. The drivers were experienced and there were very few accidents with the racecars continually whizzing around the track. There was considerable skill involved and, believe it or not, many paying spectators did not appreciate that skill. They wanted some action - spinouts, rollovers and crashes. (We really have not changed that much since watching the gladiators compete in the Roman Coliseum.) As a result, there was a gradual evolution to racing modified stock cars. These were assembly line cars, "souped up" to race. The drivers were good, but there was a little more bumping and jostling for position, resulting in an occasional crash to satisfy the base instincts of the crowds. However, it was not long before the folks in the stands got bored with that, and more action was required to keep those seats filled.

That is where the Duke entered the picture. My good friends Bob and Dick Rossman, who had lived down the street from me in Rosedale where we grew up (we even shared a party line telephone) wanted to compete in the new class of cars racing at Freeport. The Novice class. (These cars bore the prefix A. My number was A138.) They were unmodified (except for safety features) stock cars, driven by anybody willing to get behind the wheel. Now it seems that that was the hitch with the Rossman brothers. They loved cars, were excellent mechanics, and had a car they wanted to race, but were not too anxious to get behind the wheel.

"Hey Bill, how would you like to…..?"

Why not? I had as much racing experience as the other novice drivers. Zero. This lack of experience meant there was lots of action when we raced. And that was what the crowd wanted. So the novice cars would race alternate heats with the modified stocks. There would be preliminary heats in both categories, followed by semi-finals and then the night was capped with the final races.

Driving was exciting. After getting the green flag to start the race, the floor-mounted gearshift would be locked into second gear using a heavy-duty hook attached to the dashboard. Engines roared, tires screeched and the smell of burning rubber filled the stadium. Top speed was 45 to 50 mph, but it felt like 90 mph. The small quarter mile track meant the straightaways were very short and after coming out of one turn you almost immediately went into the next one. The cars skidded, spun-out and crashed. The crowds loved it and so did I!

On one other occasion I flipped the car over, the race was halted and a there was a replay by the announcer of my earlier incident. But don't think they were the only accidents I was in. Crashes occurred on a regular basis and many nights I exited the track behind a tow truck. During one race I rammed another car's rear bumper, spun it out and ended its race. The driver came looking for me in the pits after the race and I had to explain to him, "Hey man, it was an accident. Didn't do it on purpose, man. You know what I mean, man?" (That was the lingua franca of the day.) He grumbled a few choice epithets and stalked away.

I should really say something about my fellow participants in this – new for me – sport of stock car racing. The modified drivers, their pit crews and friends tended to be blue-collar types. Skilled mechanics, hard workers, guys with families. In general the novice drivers did not quite make it up to those standards. I would like to think of the Rossman's and me as anomalies among the greasy looking, dirty, unshaven, leather jacketed members of this bunch. But my memory is not so good, and maybe they were really good, clean-cut college types.

I do not have a case full of trophies and my winnings were meager. Probably twenty dollars was my biggest prize. But there was one time I won a semi-final race and after receiving the checkered flag and completing my victory lap, three burly stewards walked over to the car, and with me still inside, tipped it up enough to inspect the suspension. (As I said before novice cars were allowed no modifications.) Now it seems that Bob and Dick had illegally strapped the left side of the car body down to the chassis to prevent it from leaning excessively to the right during turns. Who would ever find out? Well, these men did, and the announcer once again mentioned my name to the multitudes. "Ladies and gentlemen, Duke Domjan's car has been disqualified from the race because of illegal suspension". As I drove off the track, boos and catcalls filled the air. I had stumbled again, but at least I was getting some form of recognition.

THE NEW CAR

I was 27 years old, the car was brand new and paraphrasing an old commercial it was a, "Melody in metal a symphony in steel."

1959 Plymouth Belvedere

I t was 1959, I was an engineer at the Sperry Gyroscope Company, belonged to the Sperry Ski Club and was in the position to buy a new car for the first time in my life. Life was good! This was the era of the tail fins and looking back, those cars were truly grotesque. However, at the time the American auto manufacturers were competing as to who could have the largest fins. My Plymouth sedan, with moderate size fins, was everything I ever wanted. Two-door sedan, seated six, plenty of power, standard transmission and a trunk big enough to fit my nearly seven foot skis, with room for golf clubs and even a basketball. But, most of all, it was brand new.

I would have it one year.

During the winter of 1959-60 most weekends were spent skiing with either the Sperry Ski Club, which I had just joined, or with my other non-Sperry friends. I used my car whenever possible and it was ideal. Spring and summer came and I would occasionally go out with Sue, a local Floral Park girl. Sue was a very attractive blonde, slightly built, but with an unusual capacity to consume liquor. She could consume copious amounts of alcohol without any outward affect. I was a mere mortal - a few drinks could be tolerated but after that, my brain became addled and my face wore a silly grin. However, neither Sue nor I were much in the conversation department, so by busily drinking whiskey (Sue) and beer (me) we spent many a pleasant evening together. That was Sue.

The Party/the aftermath

At about the same time I became very friendly with Charlie Thompson, a fellow Sperry employee. We hit it off right from the start and went on many ski trips together as well as to local dances (just about every Friday there was a dance sponsored by a ski club, Young Republican Club or some other group). Charlie also knew some of the students I had met while going to Hofstra a few years earlier, including Bob Concannon and his brother Dick. (aside: Dick Concannon eventually married the daughter of Wellington Mara an owner of the New York Giants football team). Dick was living with some other young urban professionals (the term "yuppie" had yet to be coined) in Woodside, Queens and was having a BYOB party; he invited Charlie and me.

Sue was my date. By bringing my own bottle, the cost of keeping us supplied with drinks would be reduced and conversation would be easier in a large group. Sue liked vodka, I could tolerate it if mixed with orange juice (or so I thought), and a quart of the stuff is what I bought. With my purchase came a small booklet, "How to Have a Vodka Party". It should have included the word, "Not".

Saturday night I picked up Sue and drove into Woodside with my bottle of spirits, still in its brown paper bag along with the party booklet. As you may know, when vodka is mixed with orange juice, our taste buds just register juice while the brain just registers alcohol. After imbibing for many hours my gray matter was pretty soggy. When we left Dick's apartment early Sunday morning, Sue was in no better shape – but she was not driving. Remember, in 1960 there were no seatbelts, there was no MADD, there was no SADD; however, there were many drivers that were just plain BADD (badly affected drunk drivers). I was one of them.

I was driving (or at least I was seated in the driver's seat) on the Long Island Expressway that was then under construction on the former Horace Harding Blvd. Then it happened - my practically brand new car (it was only a year old) hurtled up a huge pile of recently excavated earth, rolled over in midair and came crashing down on the roof, the windshield splattering before my bloodshot eyes. For a few brief seconds - with the splintering glass, the crunching of metal, the feeling of being tossed around in the car – I did not know what was happening. When the car stopped, Sue and I were lying on the ceiling, amazingly unscratched, and very much wide-awake. We crawled from the wreck and were quickly surrounded by other people that pulled off the road – some to offer assistance and others to just gawk.

Soon the police arrived and then an ambulance. Telling them we were OK and trying to be as articulate as possible, we dismissed the ambulance. Not so the police. In response to their request for my registration I opened my car's trunk that now opened down instead of up. (I did not like carrying a bulging wallet in my pocket - did not have credit cards then and kept cash in my pockets - and the trunk seemed a logical place to keep the wallet with my license and registration just in case I ever needed them. I did not expect this would be the reason for needing them.) However, there were a number of objects in the trunk that fell to the ground. One was my basketball, that began to roll down the Long Island Expressway. In my altered state of mind, rescuing that ball was my highest priority. So down the road I staggered to retrieved that loose ball. Then the wallet. The police eventually recorded the necessary information and someone offered to drive us back to Floral Park. My car would be left there, as it was not blocking any traffic; it was safely off the road laying on its roof.

At that time, I was living in Floral Park, in an apartment over the Tulip Hill Bowling Alley, with my sister Marge and her two young daughters. Upon awakening the next morning, I had a bone-crushing headache and the feeling that something terrible had happened. Then I remembered. "Oh my God, what do I do now?" For starters, go back to the scene of the crime. I called my two good friends, Charlie

Thompson and Bob Johnson, explained the situation and asked them to drive me back to Woodside. My three and four years old nieces overheard the conversation and went whooping and hollering back to their mother screaming delightedly, "Uncle Billy turned his car upside down, Uncle Billy turned his car upside down".

The Picture

Later that Sunday, Charlie, Bob and I looked over the wreck. I was sick to my stomach and it was not all hangover. Next to the car was my booklet "How to Have a Vodka Party". I could add another chapter to that. Then Charlie started taking pictures and insisted I do a handstand in front of the car. Said it would make a great picture with both of us upside down. "No Charlie, please, my head is splitting, I'm about to throw up and I feel just plain rotten". But Charlie persisted and the picture was taken. Shortly after, two little old ladies who lived nearby, came by the wreck and asked if anybody had been hurt. When I said there were no injuries, one woman nodded knowingly and said, "Ah, they must have been good Cath-olics".

A few days later an insurance adjuster called (I had filed a claim – the vehicle was totaled) inquiring about any passengers that might have been injured. Now I had spoken to Sue earlier (we went out the night after the accident) and she had gone to the doctor because her head hurt so badly. His examination indicated no concussion, just a terrible hangover. I only told the adjuster of the visit but not the diagnosis and indicated Sue would like to be reimbursed for her full medical expenses. "How much?" he asked. "The full $10 doctor's fee", I replied. (Remember this was 1960). He immediately called Sue and offered her $100 for her signature on a release. She signed - and that was one happy adjuster.

A few months later, I attended a Motor Vehicle Bureau hearing and had my license suspended for thirty days for failure to maintain control of an automobile. But that is not the end of the story. It did not end for another 36 years because of "the picture" – the 35mm slide that Charlie took of the car and me.

As time went on the whole episode became sort of a joke. However, after having children (being old fashioned Barbara and I got married first) I certainly did not want this to set an example for them while growing up, and it was never mentioned in their company. In the meantime I had never seen Charlie's slide, and although I would ask occasionally, he would just say, "Yeah I'll find it one of these days".

The years went by, the kids grew up, and when they really learned to drive – that is, after their first accidents, which are inevitable – I told them of my misadventure. I also told them of the picture. After that, whenever my daughter Bobbi saw Uncle Charlie, she asked about the picture and he told her what he always told me, "Yeah, one of these days". She even had Charlie as an instructor at Farmingdale College one summer and repeatedly pestered him about it. But with no results.

Then at my son Stephen's wedding reception in 1996, Charlie made a presentation – not to Stephen and his wife Pamela – but to Bobbi, of a poster size blowup of her father standing on his hands in front of his 1959 Plymouth standing on its roof. It had been 36 years since that photo was taken and by this time I was not sure it had ever existed. Another shot was then taken of me standing on my hands (with assistance this time) next to the picture.

Me and 1959 Plymouth Belvedere

This was not a stumble, it was a full-blown fall and the infamous picture now hangs in my study.

MAN OF THE YEAR

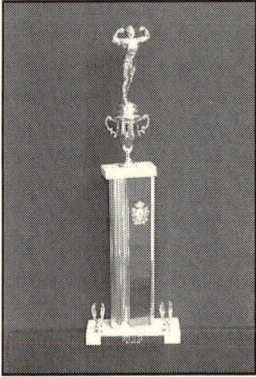

It was an unusual year.

In 1975 I was working as a traffic engineer for the Sperry Gyroscope Company in Great Neck, New York. Sperry was a good place to work. The job was interesting (designing computerized traffic control systems) and the people I worked with were cooperative and friendly. What I remember most vividly is the gym.

Weight Lifters Club

The company was originally founded by Elmer Sperry in the early 1900s, and the Great Neck plant, built during WWII, was a huge sprawling facility combining both manufacturing and engineering. The half-mile long building regularly used tricycles for transportation of men and materials down the main aisle (called Broadway). Shortly after it opened a group of shop workers convinced company management to provide some weight lifting equipment and a place to use it during their lunch break. And so was born the Sperry Weight Lifters Club. Stories are told that these guys were good, competed against other clubs, and some men (it was only men back then) actually came to work at Sperry just to join the club. However, as time went on the club disbanded and the gym was seldom used.

Jogging Craze

Then in the 1970s the running craze began. Monthly running magazines saturated the newsstands with articles on the top track athletes and included tips on how to improve your own individual performance. Jim Fixx wrote a best seller on running (and then died of a heart attack while running one morning a few years later). But the most important change was the development of new running shoes. No longer thin soled sneakers with no support, these were shoes with thick cushioned soles, arch supports and leather tops. As pocket calculators replaced slide rules, the new jogging shoes replaced sneakers, and Sperry engineers started jogging around the plant during lunch, using the rundown lockers and showers of the old weight lifters gym.

Sperry Athletic Club

As time went on more people became interested in running and physical fitness, and this resulted in the reincarnation of the Sperry Weight Lifters Club as the Sperry Athletic Club (SAC). Once again the club convinced the company to improve the facilities. More equipment was purchased with SAC dues and company funds, and a series of awards were set up for various levels of athletic achievement. There was a Level I Award for doing 15 pull-ups and Level II for 20 pull-ups. There was a Man of the Month award that had no special requirements except no one could "win" the award more than once. This resulted in many receiving it because of longevity and good attendance rather than any great physical prowess. There were also running awards given annually.

At the end of the year SAC had a big luncheon for all members, with trophies given to these award winners. The trophies stood on an awards table prior to the official ceremony, each with the recipient's name on them - except for one. It was the largest trophy of all and only the SAC executive committee knew who would receive it. The award was for – Man of the Year.

This was all in place when in 1972 I came back to Sperry after spending eight years at Grumman on the Apollo Lunar Landing program. My lunch period was from 11:48 AM to 12:30 PM (42 minutes or .6 hours) and started with the ringing of a bell. Many of my co-workers would head for the gym while others went to the cafeteria or ate brown bag lunches at their desk. I soon joined the gym gang and before long, I became addicted to jogging and exercise. Like one of Pavlov's dogs, when that bell rang I automatically left my desk and started for the gym (however, I did not salivate). I became an OK runner but not great, entering many of the local races (still have not worn out all those race tee shirts) while some of the other club members regularly entered the Boston and New York City marathons. I did some exercises along with the jogging but never really excelled compared to the muscular weightlifters. I was what you would call a journeyman gym rat.

The 1975 Awards

The year 1975 was a strange one (maybe the planets were in special alignment or maybe it was a grand once-in-a-lifetime misalignment). I had been going to the gym almost every day for the past three years and apparently they had run out of men for Man of the Month - so I received that award. Then I managed to squeeze out fifteen pull-ups, qualifying me for the Level I Award. There was also an award for running a certain distance within a certain time (I forget the details). Anyway, I got that award also. Now many people had received these awards over the years, but by some strange quirk of fate, I got them all in the same year - 1975.

That December, I went to the SAC annual luncheon and picked up my Level I, Man of the Month, and Running trophies. Never having been especially accomplished in any sport, going home with this loot was a real ego booster. However, after all the awards, but one, were presented (and there were plenty) everyone wondered who the big winner would be. Would it be one of the sculpted-body muscle men that weight lifted every day, or one of the runners that ran the Boston

Marathon? Or maybe someone who did both - whose body was well defined from moderate weight lifting, but who also placed well in the local races?

Drum roll, please. With much fanfare the president of the Sperry Athletic Club announced the winner of 1975's Man of the Year award - Bill Domjan. The 1974 winner then presented me with this huge trophy, pictures were taken by the Sperry News photographer and in a dumbfounded state I returned to my table.

Post Script

Nobody that I know ever complained about it, but there were times when I would be introduced as - Bill Domjan, man of the year - in a somewhat sarcastic tone. But that's OK, there are no asterisks in the SAC record book. Maybe I had stepped in something, but I did not stumble.

Bill ??, me and Mike Gentile (1974 Man of Year)

OF BACKACHES, CHIROPRACTORS AND OTHER 21ST CENTURY SNAKE OIL

Now it is called homeopathic medicine.

The other day while looking for something in one of my junk filled dresser drawers I found ankle, wrist and elbow tapes, a lace-up ankle support, all-purpose elastic bandages, orthotics, Dr. Scholl's heel lifts, Preparation H and a metal thumb protector. That got me to thinking. Downstairs in the kitchen cabinet are jars of glucosium sulphate, saw palmetto tablets, and multi-vitamins. None really worked – they were nothing but Snake Oil! However, the biggest fraud I ever encountered was the chiropractor I had visited a few of years ago. His mantra was, "remember you might feel well but you are not, so continue to come for your subluxation adjustments".

Years ago there were salesmen that traveled the country in their horse drawn wagons selling elixirs alleging to cure all your ills, from diarrhea to constipation and everything in between. However, those guys were honest healers compared to the claims of chiropractors who say that most illnesses can be cured through regular spinal adjustments. Now I am not about to describe and deride every phony claim they make, but a little history of my aching back might illustrate the skepticism I have for this profession (as well as for some medical doctors, homeopathic medicine, most over-the-counter drugs, many prescription drugs, megavitamins and other magical elixirs).

Sometime around 1946 (at age 14) I was trying to flip over Jackie Reynold's back and in the process landed on my head. I think that was what started my back problem, but who knows? Anyway, while going to Hofstra College a few years later my back started to act up and although I could not stand up straight for a month, I just kept hobbling around until it got better. (Realization came thirty years later - after undergoing many quack treatments - this was probably the best cure.) In fact one time it went "out" (I don't know what "out" means but I know how it feels) just before I was to go skiing with Bob Martin at Mohawk Mountain in Connecticut. I went anyway and just skied in the Quasimoto position.

Most of the time over the years my back has felt reasonably normal, but periodically it does acts up. Here is a little history of the "cures" I have tried.

Picking up my two-year old son Joseph, I felt a strange sensation in my lower back and within two hours back spasms made me a hopeless cripple unable to stand straight and barely able to hobble around because of the pain. I went to Doctor G. (names are not mentioned to protect the guilty) and his diagnosis was that it was a worn disk in the lower back that might require spinal fusion. However, he did offer a ray of hope - his father had a similar problem, but his vertebrae had naturally fused by the time he reached sixty. Spinal fusion, or wait thirty years - some choice! Instead I was fitted for an elaborate back brace that looked like an 18th century woman's corset. At times I have worn it and still have it, but it never relieved the pain or hastened healing. I also never went back to Doctor G.

The next time it went out, I went to an orthopedic surgeon, Doctor M. He told me it was just a muscle pull and not to worry about it. (He was probably too busy with ailments that could be treated – not backaches that are as common as the common cold and just about as curable). I felt he was just ignoring my problem, but looking back maybe he was the first one to get it right. It did eventually return to normal.

After the next episode I went to Doctor S., the back doctor. He told me it was a muscle pull that would respond to anti-inflammatory medication and physical therapy. I took the medicine and went for therapy. The sessions were twice a week for two months and they included whirlpools, massage, ultrasound, ice and special swimming pool exercises. It wasted my time and the insurance company's money, but it did eventually get better (long after the therapy ended).

The next time I bent over the wrong way I visited Doctor S. again. This time he prescribed chiropractic treatment. Now the chiropractor I saw must have been a direct descendent of an original nineteenth century snake oil salesmen.

"I'll tell you what I'm gonna' do. You come for my regular treatment of subluxation adjustments for just a limited time (say the rest of your life) and I will maintain your extremely sick back that has numerous degenerative, herniated, blown out, slipped discs" (as he showed me the results of my extensive and expensive X-rays).

I started at three times a week for two months with treatment consisting of 15 minutes of ultrasound (I was left unattended in a room with an ultrasonic device strapped to my back while the doctor was "adjusting" other patients) followed by a five minute session on a chiropractic couch where the good doctor would crack my back and neck like a gigantic set of knuckles. (I later read that some people had been paralyzed by an over-zealous neck snap.) I had to argue with him to get down to two treatments a week (he constantly reminded me how sick I was, no matter how good I felt). Eventually I got fed up with this charlatan and quit going despite repeated phone calls from his office. The only thing worthwhile from the experience was a cheap ballpoint pen with a crook in it. That pen represented two things - the crook in my back and the crook trying to fix it.

I also tried a number of self-help cures obtained from books and videos (and there are plenty). I did partial sit-ups (full sit-ups are bad for the back), stretched my hamstrings (tight hamstrings are bad for the back) and tightened my stomach muscles when walking to take the arch out of my back (naturally, an arch is bad for the back). When traveling to work on the train I placed a small board behind me to keep my back properly aligned. I placed a large board under my mattress and only slept on my side to keep my back properly aligned. I hung by my legs from a chinning bar to uncompress my disks.

It was all Snake Oil.

Then came the epiphany. I read a short article from the federal government (yes Virginia, sometimes our taxes are put to good use). A review of numerous scientific studies showed that 90 percent of backs that had "gone out", completely healed by themselves in one to two months. No special treatment was required and the best treatment was to do nothing. Just try to maintain a normal schedule of eating, sleeping and working, and don't baby yourself. And guess what – it works. Periodically my back goes out and I feel miserable, but I grin and bear it and within a month it is back to normal.

And now I know why so many books on the subject have been written; why so many braces, devices and medications have been sold; and why chiropractors get so many repeat customers. Most backs heal within a month or so, with or without taking any special action. Since our backs heal no matter what the treatment, we then swear by whatever treatment we tried. When all that treatment really was – *you know what.*

SUNDAY MORNINGS AT THE BEACH

Summers on Long Island

It is Sunday morning and I'm sitting by the ocean, drinking coffee and eating bagels as I watch my two grandsons play in the surf. Sitting with me is my wife of 39 years, my son and his wife, and many of my Greenlawn neighbors. Today there are eighteen of us, last week there were about ten. Other Sundays, Barbara and I might be the only ones. It is a ritual that has been ongoing for over 25 years.

It all started many years ago when one of our friends suggested that some Sunday morning we cook breakfast at the Field 5 picnic area of Robert Moses State Park. A few of us met there with our charcoal, bacon, eggs, juice and all the necessary ingredients for a picnic breakfast. It took a while to get everything prepared, but sitting at that picnic table, smelling the salt air and sizzling bacon while watching the kids play, and hearing the pounding surf was a sensory delight. (And at nearby tables there were some older couples - we were young then - having a champagne breakfast.) Breakfast over, we headed for the beach a few short yards away, and enjoyed the surf and sun for the next few hours. By noon we had soaked up our quota of UV rays and left for home. The day had been so successful we continued this routine Sunday after Sunday for the next few summers.

What kept us together was probably that we were all friends living in the Greenlawn area with common interests centered around our young children. Harborfields schools, Boy Scouts, Girl Scouts and sports kept us actively involved with our kids and each other.

As time passed the preparation of elaborate beach breakfasts became a chore and our eating habits gradually evolved into hot coffee and bagels taken directly to the water's edge. There are some variations – doughnuts, juice, fruit – but the main staple is bagels and java. Certain rituals also evolved. Like dipping into the Atlantic prior to breaking our fast (breakfast). On an August day with water temperatures in the mid-seventies this is not a big deal. On Memorial Day weekend with the water temperature below sixty degrees this can be an outer body experience. In those early days, Frank Springer and I considered this our physical for the year. If we did not get a heart attack when the shock of frigid water hit our chest like a sledgehammer, we were good for another year.

As time went on, people moved, kids grew up and life changed. But there were always a few that would go to Robert Moses, Field 5 and set up their beach chairs in the same spot - near the lifeguard stand, just to the right of the green flag. Although sometimes no one was there and at other times there were only one or two couples – the tradition lingered on. Now there is a resurgence of interest and our grandchildren have discovered the joy of the beach on an early Sunday morning. On most mornings I try to maintain the tradition of bathing before breakfast but I did stop taking my unofficial Memorial Day ocean physical. I now take a more traditional exam, as in 1994 I had a quadruple bypass (must have been the year I stopped taking my Robert Moses survival test).

MAINE HIGH ADVENTURE

A weeklong canoe trip in the wilderness

The low rumbling sound of the rapids could be heard long before they became visible. Tony Daniel, in the lead canoe with Tracy Reynolds, motioned for us to follow him to the riverbank. We beached our five canoes and followed Tony through the thick woods to an opening where we could see the river as it dropped through a series of ledges, rocks and chutes to quieter water downstream. Tony described the best route down through this maize of obstacles before he walked back to his canoe and put the plan into action. We watched in admiration as he skillfully used a combination of draw, pull and pry strokes to negotiate his way down the cascading river.

This was our introduction to real white water canoeing as we began our five-day wilderness canoe trip through the remote forests, lakes and streams of Baxter State Park in northern Maine. Six months in the planning, we were now starting our Boy Scout High Adventure. Eight teenagers (including my sons Joseph and Stephen) from Troop 225, Greenlawn, NY and me, along with Tony our twenty-year old guide would be traveling 65 miles on a series of lakes and rivers in this wilderness area. It was far different from any canoeing we had done on the Delaware River in New Jersey. We would be living for five days in complete isolation from the civilized world. Everything needed would be carried in the canoes – tents, sleeping bags, clothing, food. And the canoes would not always be in the water. There would be nine portages, some more than a mile, through dense woods, swampy ground and swarming with bugs. The days would be long, our feet would be constantly wet and at the end of each day our muscles would ache. We would have a great time.

Getting there

Our trip started from my house on a Friday night in a large van loaded down with camping gear and eight high-spirited Boy Scouts (mostly sixteen year olds). The first night was spent at Fort Devens, Massachusetts where tents were set up under the glare of headlights, for a brief overnight stay. In the morning, after breakfast in the army mess hall, we continued north. There was a brief stop at L.L. Bean in Freeport, Maine where their round-the-clock department store operation was in stark contrast to the mom and pop stores that made up the rest of the business district this day in 1981. Then on to Matagamon, where we spent the second night at a private campground, across the lake from the High Adventure base camp.

Sunday morning the boys made a breakfast of eggs with sausage that would be our last "real meal" for the next week. Leaving the van, we were ferried across to the base camp where we met our guide, Tony. Wearing a crushable hat on tousled blonde hair, and a faded scout uniform on a slight frame, I thought my rugged crew of testosterone-loaded teenagers might be too much for him. I was wrong. This young man, who would be an intimate member of our crew for the next five days, was truly a unique person – a scout among scouts. Skilled in the ways of camping, fishing, canoeing and outdoor living in general, he was also knowledgeable of the geology, and plant and animal life in the area. He had boundless energy and strength (he was the only one of the ten of us that could single handedly portage a canoe) and although his voice was never louder than conversational, he did not take long to gain complete respect of the entire crew. When Tony spoke, we listened.

Preparations

That Sunday we spent preparing for our high adventure. Stephen, the oldest boy at seventeen, had been elected crew chief and the boys told him they were interested in white water canoeing, Samoa boating, rump bumping and hiking. Meeting with the base camp director and using U.S. Geologic Survey maps, a 65 mile trip was mapped out that would take us on a series of lakes and rivers through varied terrain in the Maine north woods.

Drawing out the necessary equipment and food supplies (lots of freeze-dried stuff), we set up camp, with Tony going through the standard procedures that would be followed each day. He showed us how to pack and unpack our canoes quickly and efficiently and how to make our packs watertight (a necessity when shooting rapids). He reviewed the procedures for setting up and breaking camp; after beaching and securing the canoes, teams would be assigned to various chores that included starting the campfire, soaping the outside of the pots for easier cleaning (cooking was over open fires), digging a latrine and preparing dinner. After dinner another team would clean up. Efficiency and teamwork were the watchwords as there would be long days spent in the canoes and there was no time to be wasted at the campsites.

The next morning we packed our canoes, paddled them across the lake, loaded them onto a trailer, hopped into the van towing them and headed onto a logging road leading deep into the dense Maine woods. After more than an hour we reached the drop off point, unloaded the canoes and started our journey.

Samoa Boats and Rump Bumping

One morning after breaking camp we set out in the canoes for a small tributary that came down through a series of rock ledges and small water falls to meet the river. It was not navigable for a canoe but with an inflatable Samoa boat and wearing life jackets and crash helmets, up to four people would get an exciting ride down through this turbulent stream. It was like a flume ride at an amusement park only more exciting and it was for real. Two, three or four scouts would carry the boat upstream to a relatively quiet spot, enter the water, paddle a few strokes and then hang on for dear life as they flew down through the raging, tumbling chaos of white water.

After everyone had completed a few runs in the Samoa boat, it was time to rump bump this same route. The name is self-descriptive and to protect our rumps we wore a second life jacket with our legs through the armholes – it resembled a large gray diaper. Wearing this along with a crash helmet, we entered the water further upstream than before, where even a Samoa boat could not survive. Feet pointed downstream, arms outstretched, and frequently dunked, we flew down through the turbulence laughing and screaming. Toward the end of the ride there was a spot where you would be sucked under water and then pop up about fifty feet downstream. It was exhilarating.

Sailing

On another morning, while preparing to leave a lakeside campsite, Tony announced we would do some sailing. The wind was blowing in the right direction so we lashed our five canoes together side by side, made a makeshift mast from our tent poles and hoisted our dining fly sail. It was a sunny day with beautiful views of the unspoiled Maine wilderness and a pleasant break from the seemingly endless paddling done each day. However, it was only for a few miles and then it was back to our human powered propulsion.

Portages

There were nine portages over the course of the trip. Some were over a mile, all required two trips (one for the canoes and one for the backpacks) and the terrain was less than hospitable. None of us, except Tony, could carry a canoe single-handed and in general, two of us would carry one canoe with our heads inside. This was the easiest way, but visibility was limited. As we stumbled through the woods there were times when a tree would be whacked and our ears would ring (it was like being on the inside of a drum).

Rapids

We had experienced rapids before in our many trips canoeing the Delaware River, but never so many and so difficult as here in Maine. For some of the more difficult stretches of water we would stop upstream, beach the canoes, reconnoiter the conditions and plan a route down through them. This did not guarantee success.

On one three-mile stretch of rock gardens, Steve and John capsized three times, Joseph and Brad twice, and Pat and I once. On another occasion, Brad went after a lost cushion and almost body surfed down a series of ledges we were to portage around. Bruising his arm and thumb it was difficult paddling for a while after. There was not a day that went by that someone did not capsize. Having watertight packs and knowing how to recover made a potentially hazardous experience just a minor inconvenience. However, I did lose a paddle on one overturn (it cost me $5) and used a spare one after that.

Campsites

Each day, late in the afternoon, we would arrive at our preplanned campsite. Scouts regularly used these as they canoed through this area. There would be sufficient open area for our tents and there would be a small stack of firewood to be used and later replenished. We were always overlooking a lake or river with breathtaking views of the surrounding countryside. Some mornings there would be a light fog creating a surrealistic scene until it burned off shortly after sunrise. We went to bed early, slept soundly and were up early – between 5 and 6 AM - to prepare breakfast and break camp. It was not exactly mom's home cooking but there were never any leftovers (the many calories expended each day had to be replenished). We would be on the river within two hours of arising.

Final Thoughts

After five days on the river it was good to get back to civilization and take a hot shower. It had been a great adventure, but we are really all city slickers unaccustomed to living in the outdoors without our support system that we take for granted – hot water, stoves, refrigerators, television, solid roofs over our head, flush toilets ...and the list goes on. The days had been long, our feet had been wet and our muscles still ached. But you know what - after it was over we all felt a little bit better about ourselves.

MAINE HIGH ADVENTURE
July, 1981

CREW
(back row)
Tom Dowling
Lee Papageorge
Bill Domjan
Joe Domjan
Brad LeBaige
Tony Daniel
(front row)
Steve Domjan
John Sarcona
Tim Madigan
Tracy Reynolds

SKIING

Skiing 101

S ometime in the mid-1950s I was introduced to Alpine (downhill) skiing. Now skiing is an activity and only an activity. It is not a way of life. It does not build moral character; it is not even a good aerobic exercise. However, it does build strong quadriceps and in the spring you can get a nice tan. I have been doing it each winter for over fifty years. This is the story of my first time on skis.

Ray Brennan, Bob Martin and I had gone to the Jug End Barn resort in South Egremont, Massachusetts for a winter weekend of trying to meet girls. As part of the weekend, we rented skis from Jug End, and were taken to the nearby Dutch Hill ski area. We did not know anything about skiing and I mean anything. We did not know the difference between beginner or expert slopes. We did not know anything about ski lifts or how to use them. We did not know ski techniques as elementary as the snowplow. I mean, how difficult could it be? We found out. Plenty!

Dutch Hill was not a big area but it did have a main T-bar lift that went to its summit and had some fairly difficult trails coming down. There were other lifts serving the novice and beginner trails but we were not aware of them, so the T-bar it was. T-bars look like upside down Ts attached to an overhead loop of cable that continuously brings skiers up the hill, two at a time. Pairs of skiers shuffle into the path of the T-bar after it rounds the turn from coming down and starts heading up again. An attendant hands the T-bar to the skiers who grab the stem of the T with their inside hands. They then lean back and let the T-bar pull them up the slope. The secret is to *not* sit on the T-bar but just lean back. We did not know the secret, at least not Ray and I.

Bob went up first with someone familiar with the lift and had no problem (also maybe he was better coordinated). Ray and I were next. We grabbed the T-bar, sat down and fell off. We tried again and fell again. Each time we fell, the lift operator shut the lift down until we struggled/crawled out of the way of the skiers next in line. This is no mean feat when we could hardly walk on these huge boards no less try to recover from a fall. This happened two or three times and we were getting exhausted while the lift operators and skiers waiting in line were getting exasperated. We still did not know there were easier lifts and easier areas of the mountain to ski. The next time on the lift, Ray and I fell again but this time I hung onto the T-bar as it dragged me up the mountain. People were yelling to let go but I figured this was probably going to be the only way I would ever make it to the top. Poles were dropped along the way but were retrieved by others coming up the lift. Bob was patiently waiting as I arrived encrusted in snow and Ray eventually joined us.

If it was this difficult getting up the mountain using a ski lift, you can imagine the problems coming down. We had been so busy just trying to learn to walk on these contraptions that we hadn't given much thought to steering them downhill. We just thought that everybody who learned to ski started on trails like these.

We watched others skiing but really could not figure out what they were doing to control their skis; how could we learn by watching, when just standing was a challenge. So we developed our own special technique. Point the skis in the desired downhill direction, struggle to a standing position, ski down until the trail starts to turn and then fall down. Repeat this until the bottom is reached and then get on the lift and start all over again. It wasn't until that night at dinner when reviewing the day's events with others that we realized we had been on the expert slopes all day. Oh my God, we had surely stumbled!

As I said before skiing is not a way of life and does nothing to improve your moral character, but that one day on skis got me hooked. It has remained a source of outdoor winter enjoyment for me and my family ever since.

TUCKERMAN'S RAVINE

Skiing the Steeps

Tuckerman's Ravine is a glacial cirque and a part of Mt. Washington, New England's highest peak. As a rite of spring, each year skiers from the Northeast trek to this readily accessible area for some end-of-season skiing. Although easy to get to, it is not for the faint hearted. There are no lifts and it requires a two to three hour hike from the parking lot at Pinkham Notch, up a muddy, slippery trail just to get to the base of the ravine. And then the real fun begins. With skis over one shoulder, you start the near vertical climb up the ravine (at least it seems that way, especially since you can reach straight out and touch the snow with your hand). After close to an hour of exhaustion mixed with fear you decide this is enough - let me put my skis on and get this over with. You pack down sufficient snow to make a platform large enough to set the skis on, and then look back at where you came from. This is where you will soon be going – but at a much greater speed.

Below are lines of skiers trailing in each other's footsteps, looking like a string of ants in the distance, as they plod up the slopes. The weather is mild – it is the Memorial Day weekend – and water can be heard running beneath the snowy surface. Waterfalls spring out of the steepest slopes and there is the occasional crevasse created in the wet slippery snow that can drop a skier 30 feet or more to the bedrock below. Now push off from the sanctity of the makeshift platform and head down the steeps. Going straight down is not advisable as speeds over 100 mph can be reached (at one time ski speed records were set at Tuckerman's). Quick turns are required and prayers that you do not fall, although not required, are sometimes invoked. In less than two minutes you are at the base and ready to start over. Four runs, or about 8 minutes of skiing represent a typical day of skiing. Although actual ski time is short, the bragging rites are forever.

I have been to Tuckerman's four times and will briefly regale my adventures.

Trip 1 - 1960

Charlie Thompson, Bob Johnson, Anne Jennerich and I arrived at the Appalachian Mountain Club (AMC) lodge at the Pinkham Notch base of Mt. Washington on the Friday night of the Memorial Day weekend. Early the next morning, after a night in the dorms, we started up the mountain. We were not just going to ski the steeps, we were also going to camp at the base of the ravine, sleeping overnight in one of the lean-tos. In addition to carrying our skis, boots and poles we also had sleeping bags, food, drink (six-packs of beer) and if that was not enough, I was going to play the part of a troubadour and brought my guitar to serenade the fair maiden Anne. I even had a kerosene lantern hanging from my overladen pack. We slowly plodded our way up the steep trail for what seemed like endless hours. When we reached the campsite, Bob with his head down and in a numbed state of mind slogged on for another half hour until realizing he was all alone. When he finally arrived back, he was quite annoyed that we had let him continue. We were too tired to know he was missing.

Although exhausted it was now time to ski. On the Lunch Rocks - an outcropping of rocks at the base of the snowy slopes - scores of skiers were relaxing and enjoying the sights and sounds of the scene around them. Also maybe having a beer sold by some rugged enterprising entrepreneur who spent many hours lugging up a case from the base of the mountain. A park ranger sat on the rocks with a bullhorn ready to announce any avalanche in progress. A consoling thought.

That day we climbed the ravine for the first time; we had never experienced anything like it. Exhausting, exhilarating, exciting and a little bit scary, especially when looking down at the start of each run. However, we managed to ski the slopes without any mishaps and felt pretty good about ourselves at the end of the day.

That evening we set about laying out our sleeping bags in the lean-to, preparing dinner and then relaxing around a campfire. I took out my guitar and was about to launch into my vast repertoire of three-chord folk songs (I knew about four – The Sloop John B, On Top of Old Smoky,...) when Pierre, from Montreal, asked if he could see the instrument. To my chagrin he knew how to play, knew more than four songs and entertained us for the rest of the evening. Adding insult to injury he borrowed Bob's plastic phone company ID card for use as a pick and returned a small nub of plastic when he was through playing. And I did not even get credit for lugging the axe up the mountain. However, I did learn one thing from Pierre. He sawed the handle off his toothbrush to save weight when backpacking. (I suspect he did not carry a kerosene lantern either.)

Trip 2 - 1963

Two major events on this trip. Jim Ansboro tried and failed to ski the steeps and I became engaged to my future wife, Barbara Blatnicky. Neither event was planned.

This time there were more of us in the group (in addition to Barbara, Jim and myself there were Betty Deagan, Bob Johnson, Art Hedler and Don MacKenzie) and we did not camp – we only carried our ski equipment up to the ravine, and hiked back to the AMC at the end of the day. Bob and I were the old pros on this trip with approximately eight minutes ski time on the Tuckerman slopes. Most of us were experienced skiers with the exception of Jim who had only been skiing for a couple of seasons. As we started our long climb, I asked him if he would be able to ski down the steepest slopes at the ravine's summit. If not, he could just tackle the lower slopes that were not as steep and there was not as far to fall. He assured us there was no problem. As we climbed higher and the pitch of the ravine increased, I repeated the question and received the same answer. Later I asked again, "Jim, are you sure you are able to handle this mountain?" Jim - now annoyed by this line of questioning – snapped off, "Don't worry I can ski it". OK, I guessed he knew what he was doing.

We eventually reached a little outcropping high up on the slopes, where we put on our skis and prepared for the descent. Jim decided to go first and we really thought he had been misjudged, he seemed so confident. He pushed off, initially heading straight down. After going about a hundred feet he attempted to turn, fell, lost one ski and started a long tumble down the slopes. We watched in awe, as Jim, like an erratic bowling ball on a steeply inclined alley, would occasionally knock down one of the skiers in the long line ascending the ravine. And then another and another. Eventually he reached the bottom without dropping into a crevasse or colliding with a rock. No broken bones but lots of bruises and scrapes especially on his legs – he was wearing shorts. Jim spent the rest of the day climbing back up to retrieve his lost ski and then carefully walking back down the ravine. The rest of us managed to get in a few runs during the remainder of the day with no other mishaps. That night after a family style dinner and a spirited swapping of the day's adventures (Jim's little escapade not mentioned), a movie was shown of skiing Tuckerman's. It was a professional flick replete with the sound effects of a crashing car every time a skier fell.

That night in the AMC lodge, Barbara, ever cautious, barricaded her door with her luggage.

The next day we drove to the top of Mt. Washington, hiked over to the ravine and then skied down the ravine one last time. Jim did not join us.

On the long ride home I decided to pop the question and it was not, "Will you drive?" It was the $64 question, the answer was "Yes" and we were married three months later.

Trip 3 – 1967

I was now in a family way – that is I had a wife and three kids - and really felt tied down (actually I felt pretty good). However, I was looking for a little adventure and my old friend and fellow Tuckerman traveler, Bob Johnson, and I decided to head up to Mt. Washington for a little spring skiing (maybe 16 minutes worth). We slept each night at the AMC lodge and left our skis at the base of the ravine after the first day of skiing; it made the hike down and then back up the next day much easier. The most memorable moment was when the ranger sitting on the Lunch Rocks shouted over his bullhorn "Avalanche, avalanche!" I was near the bottom of the slopes and looking up the ravine, I saw this huge ball of snow rolling and bouncing down towards me. Anxious to get out of the way and trying to remain totally calm, cool and collected – I fell. It finally stopped just a few feet from me. And it really was not that big, but it did have my heart pounding for a few anxious moments.

Arriving home, unshaven for the last three days, I walked into the backyard and little three-year old Stephen called to Barbara, "There is a strange man outside".

Trip 4 – 1989

My daughter, Bobbi, had just graduated from St. Michael's College and little Stephen was now big Steve. Stephen had been to Tuckerman's once before and Bobbi had heard of our trips, and being a good skier wanted to experience for herself a little steep skiing. Chris Horner, Stephen's pal and Stephanie Gould a girl Bobbi's age, who had skied with us for years at the Sperry Ski Club lodge, joined us. We stayed at a small motel in a nearby town (the AMC lodge was full) and arrived at the base of Mt. Washington early the next morning. By noon we were hiking up in the near vertical snow. Although the girls were good skiers they were amazed at the crevasses, the waterfalls sprouting from the cliffs and the absolute steepness of the slopes. The three of us climbed about three quarters of the way to the top while Stephen and Chris climbed to the summit of the headwall. (When there is no snow the headwall is truly vertical – it just does not get any steeper.)

The scene was spectacular. We were surrounded on all sides by the White Mountains, with the sun beaming down from a clear blue sky and in the distance tiny ant-like creatures climbing the slopes. There were skiers swooping down the ravine making huge traverses and screaming with delight, while other skiers in bathing suits were sunning themselves on the Lunch Rocks. It was surreal. Later as we sat relaxing on the Lunch Rocks we saw two virile young men slowly trek up the slopes with huge truck size inner tubes. It was much slower going than those climbing with skis and when they reached a point a few hundred yards up the ravine they decided to make their descent. (Now on skis great big traverses are made to keep control of speed on this steep terrain. However, tubes do not turn, they just go straight down with no speed control.) They climbed aboard their vehicles and as they slowly picked up speed those big tubes started to rumble. It was like rapidly approaching thunder, getting increasingly louder as the tubes went faster and faster. By the time they went past us they were going forty miles an hour and I

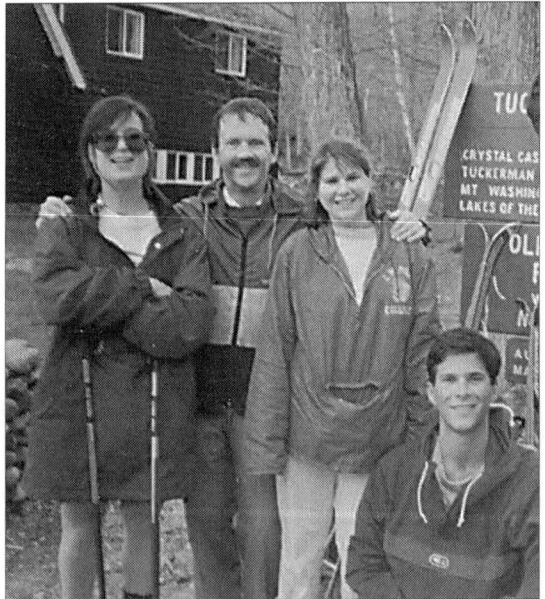

Stephanie Gould, me, Bobbi and Stephen

88

expected to see lightning with all that roaring thunder. Then their adventure came to an end. At that speed in those giant hollow doughnuts it only took a small bump to send them flying into the air and crashing into the soft snow. It was a good show.

At the end of a glorious day we hiked back down to our car, went to dinner where we relived our experiences and then back to the motel for a sound and satisfying sleep. The next day we headed back home where we would rejoin our family and friends in our existence as ordinary people living ordinary lives. However, we would always remember that day when we were "king of the hill".

THE FIRST EARTH DAY

I thought the world would join me. It did not.

As I rode my bicycle to work that day I expected to be surrounded by other riders, all proclaiming to be "one with the earth", dedicated to a "Green" way of life. Automobile drivers would be embarrassed at their wastefulness of the earth's limited resources, scorned by the endless hordes of people going to work under their own power, ridiculed for their insensitivity to the environment. After all it was April 22, 1970, the very first Earth Day.

It was later reported that two thousand colleges and universities, ten thousand primary and secondary schools, and hundreds of communities across the United States took part in that first Earth Day.

On that early spring morning in 1970, as I rode my bike on the shoulder of Pulaski Road heading for my job at Grumman Aviation, none of those tens of thousands of Earth Day supporters were on the road with me. (Maybe they were all in California – or the South Shore). Cars whizzed by me with mere inches to spare, I was obviously an intruder on their territory. I was the threat to their environment.

The day's round trip was eventually completed without mishap but with much trepidation; I never rode my bike to work again. Although I still do considerable biking on Long Island (it has many scenic and safe roads) I never ride anywhere, on any road, during the morning and evening peak traffic periods.

REX MORGAN

My fifteen minutes of fame.

"**I**'m Sergeant Tom Wagner.....". Rugged looking with thick black hair and a beard to match, Frank Springer had transformed me into a tough cop in his Rex Morgan, M.D. cartoon strip. How did this happen? It is a story.

One summer day in 1979, my good friend, backyard neighbor and professional cartoonist called on the phone.

"Bill, you want to be in one of my cartoon strips?"

"Sure, what do I have to do?"

"Hop the back fence and let me take a couple of pictures of you"

That was it until early the next year when Frank told me that detective Tom Wagner would be appearing in his Rex Morgan strip. However, there was one problem, although nationally syndicated, no New York papers carried it. Barbara called her brother Paul in Solon, Ohio and sure enough, there was Sergeant Wagner in the Cleveland Plain Dealer. Someone else saw it in the Washington Post. One weekend at the Sperry Ski Lodge in Vermont, the Strauss family, who

92

had recently moved to Boston, arrived with the Sunday edition of the Boston Globe. I asked one of their kids to check if Rex Morgan, M.D. was in the funnies. They took one look and shouted, "Mr. Domjan that's you in there!" And so it went. It was my brief 15 minutes of fame as I contacted family and friends around the country to see if my alter ego had made it to their local papers. In many cases it had.

But fame is fleeting and in a few short weeks a new plot line emerged and detective Tom Wagner, like an old soldier, just faded away. Sometime after that, the thick black hair and beard of the real world Bill Domjan also just faded away.

MACY'S THANKSGIVING DAY PARADE

I always wanted to be a clown.

Long before I was born – at least eight years anyway – the first Macy's Parade took place. The year was 1924 and it was called the Macy's Christmas Parade even though it occurred on Thanksgiving Day. It was later renamed the Macy's Thanksgiving Day Parade. As I grew up, the annual parade was not highly publicized as it is today. There was no television and a parade is not the kind of event that makes for interesting radio coverage. However, movie theaters that regularly played double features also included cartoons, previews and Movietone News. It was in these newsreels (they always ended with a movie camera facing the audience along with the words, "The eyes and ears of the world – the end") that I dimly remember pictures of the Thanksgiving Day Parade floats.

Watching the parade

I started to notice it more seriously when it was almost fifty years old. It was the early seventies and Bobbi, Stephen and Joseph would spend Thanksgiving Day morning watching the parade on TV. Aside from the tedious commercials, it was an interesting show. A few years later a good friend told me he regularly drove into the city early on parade day and watched it live. Wow! No commercials. And I had a little

Volkswagen Beetle that could squeeze into parking spots that most cars could not. So that next Thanksgiving I drove my little car filled with little people (my three kids plus their friends Stephen and John Gruinberg) into Manhattan to the parade's start at the Museum of Natural History. The kids worked their way to the curb for front row seats while I stood in the back watching them and the parade. This went on for a few years but the parking became more and more difficult, the traffic coming home became more and more congested, and the kids got older and older. We eventually stopped the annual ritual.

But that is not the end of my story.

Be clown, be a clown, be a clown

In the 1980s Barbara and I were actively involved in the Harborfields PTA Scholarship shows and one of our fellow showman was Stan Rubenstein. Stan was a nice guy, a very funny guy and a good actor. He was also a manager – of a Macy's department store. "Stan, could you possibly get me and my teenage sons to march in the Thanksgiving Day parade?"

Thursday, November 27, 1986 at 5 o'clock in the morning Stephen, Joseph and I drove into 34th Street in a cold pouring rain. In a Macy's stockroom volunteer professional makeup artists from Broadway shows were applying their art to the hundreds of parade marchers, us included. The three clowns. Now some clowns are made up with happy faces and others sad, but no makeup was needed for Joseph. His was one sad face. I don't really remember, maybe he was coerced into coming, and that combined with having to get up so early and march in the cold, miserable rain contributed to his foul mood.

The boys were handlers controlling a large Christmas ball type balloon; I was a free roaming clown waving to the crowd as I pranced down the street. When hiding behind makeup and a costume it was easy, even for me an introverted nerdy engineer, to act uninhibited. I had a great time.

The next year Stan got us into the parade once again and this time Bobbi replaced Joseph. She was on a float where she controlled the pitch and roll of a miniature plane at the top of a pole (in the plane was some minor celebrity). Stephen was enclosed in the bowels of a fire-breathing dragon, where he controlled the fiery breath. I was an engineer wearing red coveralls and rode in a "locomotive", with a rock band playing on the roof. The weather was mild and we did not even have to walk - but the thrill of that first parade just was not there.

I never went into the parade again for the next twenty years and seldom watched it on television – those commercials are more tedious than ever. However, in 2008 my brother-in-law Paul Blatnicky came into town with his family and stayed in a hotel in midtown Manhattan the night before the parade. Stephen, his two boys and I joined them. That night we watched the immense balloons being inflated in preparation for the parade the next day. The next morning we walked to Central Park West an hour before the parade start, but we were still an hour late as the crowd lining the street was at least 15 to 20 people deep. All we saw were the tops of the balloons. It was disappointing and any future parade watching will be on television – commercials and all.

CHRISTMAS LIGHTS

The season is not always jolly.

The year was 1985. Ronald Reagan was president, Iran and Iraq were at war and terrorism was on the rise. They were not my major concerns – money was my problem. My three children were all away at colleges in Vermont. Stephen was attending the University of Vermont, Joseph was at Johnson State College and my daughter Bobbi was at St. Michael's College. Years before, when I sat down and ran through the numbers, it seemed impossible to afford sending my kids away to college with all the attendant costs – and all at the same time. Yet they were going and so were all their friends. A combination of savings, student loans, my existing salary and working by the kids would just about do it. Did I say kids working? Let me tell you a story.

Going into business

My old friend Jack Howell, was always a hustler. He had been a very successful sales manager for Purolator Courier (long before Fed Ex and UPS became major deliverers) and then an entrepreneur with his own lawn service. Jack, looking for a job in the winter, hit upon the idea of providing and installing Christmas lights on private homes for the holidays. He bought hundreds and hundreds of strings of lights, did some local promoting and developed a list of about 15 customers. Now that might not sound like much, but these people paid a few hundred dollars each to have their homes decorated and the potential was there for making a few thousand dollars over the holidays. Jack did this for a few years, then sold his lawn service business and went to work at a year round job. What would he do with his Christmas decorating business and all those lights?

"Hey, Bill, I'm going out of the holiday lighting business. Would your sons be interested in making a few bucks over Christmas vacation? I'll sell you the lights for three hundred dollars, which is much less than I paid for them"

"Let me check with my sons, Jack and I'll get back to you".

Well, they were not overly enthused, but reluctantly agreed to work over vacation to help pay for their school expenses. *I should have known better.*

Jack drove to the house in his pickup truck and unloaded boxes and boxes of Christmas lights, extension cords, ribbons and various other ornaments. They filled up half my garage. Since the lights were not new they all had to be tested. And that took days and it had to be done before the boys got home, because when they arrived we had to be ready for installation. I would take each string and plug it into an outlet. Now, when two or more bulbs have burned out, none light, and each bulb must be removed separately and tested in another good string until the bad bulbs are identified. Many strings did not light, there were 50 bulbs in a string, they did not come out of the sockets easily and it was maddeningly time consuming. And I did this night after night - after coming home from my day job.

I also started calling customers to establish installation dates. It seemed that everybody wanted it done about the same time. This meant we - I use that term loosely - would have to start early each day, and work efficiently for long hours to complete all the jobs in the few weekends before Christmas. That does not really fit in with the schedule of twenty year olds who go out every night, but never before 11 PM. So most mornings, I would be up before the sun, load the car with boxes of lights, extension cords and decorations, along with my staple gun, ladder, 15 foot pole (used for placing lights on large trees) and head out to start decorating - alone.

I was up and down the ladder, stapling light strings to eves, doorframes, window boxes and anything else that would hold a staple. (My customers were not interested in aesthetics – they just wanted to have more lights than their neighbors.) Countless wreathes were hung on doors and windows (bows were made from my rolls of red ribbon and it was a struggle to keep them from looking like oversize shoelaces). Endless strings of lights encircled huge trees. It looked like a circus act as I balanced on a ladder with a 15-foot pole trying to place Christmas lights on a three-story tree. Some days were bitter cold and by the end of the day my fingers and toes would be numb. Stephen and Joseph did help, but looking back, all I remember are the times I spent alone - cursing out Jack Howell, myself, my two sons and this dumb idea.

And that was just the installation. At dinner the phone would ring. "Mr. Domjan my lights have gone out, could you come over and fix them". So over I would go – it might be a twenty minute ride – and replace the bad string, or maybe just push in the plug on the extension cords (there could be ten or fifteen on any one job). This type of complaint was not unusual and many trips were made keeping customers satisfied.

We actually made some decent money that first year and also for the next couple of years, but the procedure was always the same, with me doing all the prep work and the boys helping me - instead of the other way around, as I had hoped for. When it was time to take the decorations down the boys were back in school and that also became my job. Again, my garage would be filled with boxes.

Going out of business

Each year the job became more onerous, and the complaints more numerous - the boys had no desire to become entrepreneurs and neither did I. Each year we lost more customers and the business eventually degenerated to the point where one homeowner in Eaton's Neck told us that if we did not take his lights down soon (it was almost Easter) he would take them down himself and keep them. That was the last year of our business – he kept the lights.

Although I had stumbled again, until recently I never had to buy any Christmas lights. In fact when a string went dead I didn't even bother to fix it - just threw it away and grabbed another one. Oh, the glory of going out of business and never selling the inventory. There must be more of a moral to this story than that, but I still have not figured out what it is.

Post Script

I am told my tale is exaggerated and that my sons worked much more diligently than I have reported. My daughter also lays claim to having helped me...it is a possibility.

DOGS

Man's best friend? Sometimes.

When I was a baby we had a dog, Wanna. I only know that from an old photo showing Wanna and me in a playpen (that archaic constrictive device no longer used in our progressive – freedom now – society). Later as a kid of about ten I was allowed to keep a stray cat, Sobony, given that nom de plume by me for its physical condition when we reclaimed it from the street.

There were no more animals in my life for the next 25 years. Except for Devil, the cowardly dog, my U.S. Army platoon had as a mascot. It was a German Shepherd afraid of its own shadow - it cowered and cringed when confronted by the flea bitten little stray mongrels that hung around the barracks. But that is another story. The next significant pet to enter my life was Waffles.

The family dog

Waffles, nominally a basset hound, was more vegetable than animal. I would say all vegetable if it was not for its ability to devour food at one end and convert it into huge volumes of waste at the other. And not outside. But I'm getting ahead of myself.

Barbara and I have three children. Stephen the oldest, Joseph one year behind him and Bobbi, two years behind Joseph. When

Bobbi was about five and Leave It To Beaver, as opposed to Desperate Housewives, was the model TV family, we decided that our family of mommy, daddy and three kids was missing something. Yes, we were missing a pet dog. Also at that time there was a popular basset hound pull toy named Snoopy and we had one. So when the opportunity to buy one of these live creatures arose, we did. What a mistake!

Waffles was fairly big when we got her and she continued to grow – bigger and bigger, fatter and fatter – processing more and more food, if you get what I mean. And she never got housebroken. At night she was locked in the mudroom where the floor was lined with newspapers (I think that is when we started to read the New York Times, as the pages were larger than Newsday). Every morning I would be the first one up and would clean up the mess. But the kids loved her. She was extremely gentle – most vegetables are – and even let them dress her up in a hat and sunglasses and then be pulled around in a wagon.

However, the mudroom eventually got infested with ticks (they were living under the wallpaper) and Waffles had to be sent to "the farm". What farm? Don't ask. It was very tough for all of us and we knew it would be only a matter of time before another canine would join the family.

The designer dog

Enter Inky. This canine was not the result of some haphazard selection of any old dog - it was based on specifications demanded by Barbara. The dog could not be too big (or too small), had to be easily housebroken, reasonably intelligent, tolerant of small children and could not shed. This meant a small (15 – 20 pound) non-shedding, friendly, purebred. (A purebred, since some cute adorable puppy of unknown lineage might grow into a pony sized, child biting, continually barking, horror machine.) Inky fit the bill. She was a six week old solid black puppy whose folks were medium sized poodles (not standard poodles – too large, and not toy poodles – too small). This dog was an intimate member of the family for her 15 years of existence. The kids loved her and she loved the kids. She was low maintenance, with an occasional trip to the groomer for a haircut being the major expense. We might have placed her in a kennel a couple of times but usually grandma and grandpa (Barbara's parents) took care of her if we could not take her with us. Although she was part of our family life for many years, when she died I told my kids do not ever feel that I am lonely and need a dog as a companion. It happened to my neighbor. Karl Strombach walked that dog to the curb every morning – spring, summer, fall and winter - and then cleaned up afterward. He did it for years and I never saw him smile.

At this stage of life pets have been replaced by far more loveable and entertaining creatures – grandchildren.

SHOW BIZ

There is an old show business saying, "There are no small parts – just small people". I was one of the latter.

It all started after finishing the Dale Carnegie Course in 1970. Although I never won many friends or influenced many people, it did allow me to talk in front of a group of people without stammering, stuttering and turning every color of the rainbow. I certainly did not influence my boss at Grumman Aircraft since I was laid off shortly after receiving my Dale Carnegie certificate. However, when the Harborfields PTA and Teachers Association decided to resurrect their annual scholarship fund show, I started to think - this might be where I could practice my newly acquired skills. The show was Damon Runyon's "Guys and Dolls" and our neighbor, Barbara Springer, the show's producer was looking for crapshooters.

It was the first show the PTA/TA had produced following a teacher's strike many years earlier and community volunteers were needed. It was then I realized that even though a loner, in my heart-of-hearts I wanted to perform on stage. What made it so difficult was – that in addition to my genetic predisposition to shyness – I had very little talent. However, with my improved, but nowhere near overpowering self-confidence, I summoned the courage to read a few lines on stage and attempt to sing a few bars of some long forgotten song. My voice was – and still is – weak and without much range, but the talent pool was quite shallow that year. I was cast as Rusty Charlie, opening the show with John Shuttleworth and Joe Venuti singing, "The Fugue for Tinhorns". You know how it goes...."I've got a horse right here, his name is Paul Revere......". It was one of my biggest parts in the 25 successive years I performed in the shows.

Bill Branstin directed, Cookie Melrose starred as Adelaide and was de facto co-director. Barbara (my wife) was in the chorus along with many of our neighbors. Rehearsals lasted six weeks ending with three performances over one weekend. It was a blast! This was a new and different world, especially for a nerdy engineer. Some of these extroverted characters playing the leads were so different from my creepy (but reliable and in the end, lasting) friends. Practicing the show's songs with a choral director, blocking positions on the stage, memorizing lines (and then learning when to say them), timing of stage entrances, building sets, getting props – all for the first time.

Then to top it all off there was a cast party that included silly awards, skits, song parodies and self-congratulations. It was as much fun as the show itself.

Everything I ever learned about show business – although some may say it was not very much - I learned that year from Cookie. During the six weeks of rehearsal the show was our first priority. Her instructions: get in the proper mental state before each performance, do not meet with friends and relatives during intermission as it destroys the illusion, do not receive flowers on stage following a performance and do not rely on someone off stage feeding you lines, as there won't be anybody there. And do not look at the audience; look at the clock on the back wall.

Cookie, by the way was a short, pretty blonde with past experience performing and directing amateur theater productions. She was by no means physically overpowering, but from the first time she opened her mouth you knew she was all business, with a take-no-prisoners mentality. She directed and starred in many shows over the years and although I got to know her husband, Bob, real well (he was a nice easygoing guy) Cookie always intimidated me.

Cast Parties

The last show I had been in was Les Miserables; I played a priest from the church where Jean Val Jean stole the candlesticks. That was in the seventh grade in 1945. We may have had lemonade afterwards.

The cast party for "Guys and Dolls" was in Link's Log Cabin in Centerport, and started in the evening after the Sunday matinee show. There was lots of drinking, dancing and singing, topped off by a cast party show (more about that later). It wasn't just the alcohol we were high on, it was the thrill of being in "show business". Over the years each of the shows culminated in one of these gala parties.

For a time we had our blast at Don Steinman's home (when he moved we told the new owner there was a covenant on the house requiring it be available for the annual cast party – and it was). The parties would start after the last Saturday night's performance (we had shows Friday and Saturday on two successive weekends after the first year) and end with bagels and eggs served as the sun was rising on Sunday morning.

The highlight of the party would always be the cast party show. A few of us (never the feature performers) would get together a few days before the final show and kick around our ideas. Some people would develop skits (played by the chorus) and others songs (sung by the chorus). I would compile silly awards - everyone in the cast had to get one – that were funny but not insulting. Some were pretty good, others just plain lame. The show lasted about an hour (I was MC for many of the parties) and was always well received, as the cast was still high from the early evening applause and late evening alcohol.

This became an annual ritual in my life for 25 years. Auditions would be held sometime in January. I would dream of getting some major part, get up on the stage and bumble and stumble through a few lines from the script and wait for my cast call over the following week.

Invariably I would get a part that was less than a supporting role but slightly above the chorus level. (There is an old show business saying – there are no small parts, only small people. Well I was one of those small people. I wanted a bigger part.) There were a few - very few - times over the years when I almost reached the level of a supporting actor. I was the anvil salesman in our first "Music Man" and Mayor Shinn the second time around. On two occasions I played Pappy Yokum in "Li'l Abner". Also, over the years I was a tap dancer in "42nd Street" (I had taken tap lessons with my daughter in adult education) and a wizard in "Once upon a Mattress".

You may have guessed from the shows previously mentioned that we put on nothing but old-fashioned popular musicals. And that it was – they were all tried and true with many songs that had become popular commercial hits. We were not out to break new dramatic ground. The objective was to make money for the PTA scholarship program, and many thousands of dollars in scholarships were awarded in those 25 years. But for all the high-minded objectives, most of us were in the shows for the camaraderie, community spirit and - just plain fun.

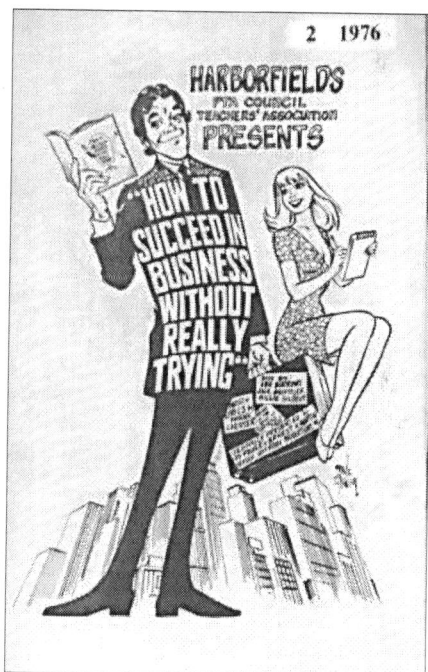

Playbill cover by Frank Springer

THE BYPASS

He said he was just a glorified plumber.

I first noticed it at the gym. I could not run around the track. No pain, but just did not have any strength or energy. It was Christmas time, 1993. Then came back and chest discomfort, not really hurtful, but nagging and persistent. After moping around on Christmas Day, Barbara got me to admit my condition and the next day I was in Dr. Gurian's office (he was covering for my regular doctor, Dr. Heller). After a quick cardiogram and stress test, he called Barbara into the office and gave us the bad news. It looked like there were severe blockages in my heart arteries and he recommended further tests (angiogram or catheterization). He also recommended that I immediately go to the hospital until the tests could be performed. Very reluctantly (and under severe pressure from Barbara) I checked into the Huntington Hospital cardiac ward.

The next day an ambulance took me to the Nassau Medical Center in Hempstead for the catheterization. Dr. Gurian was there to perform it, and after snaking the catheter from my groin up to my heart, he squirted radioactive dye into my arteries and looked at the results on a computer screen. I saw a bunch of squiggly black lines, he saw an array of biological plumbing with their life producing flow of blood being impeded by nine blockages varying from 90 to 99 percent.

My three choices

There were three alternatives and the first two were probably not viable:

1. Do nothing except take some drugs, live a very restricted life and hope for the best.

2. Undergo angioplasty (balloon surgery) where a catheter would again be inserted in the artery and a balloon at the end inflated to open the artery. About one-third of these close up in a few months and I had so many blockages it did not provide very good odds for success. (Stents, which are more effective, were not widely used at that time and I am not sure if a catheter could have reached all the blockages.)

3. Have bypass surgery, an invasive and complex procedure that would provide the most likely possibility of returning to a normal life (that for me was an active one).

I elected for number three.

The next problem was to select a hospital. I could go to Stonybrook immediately or someplace else. But where? Luckily, there had been recent articles in Newsday about the heart procedures being performed at local hospitals, and nearby St. Francis, in Roslyn, was the top one in the area. The paper also listed a box score for the different doctors there, the number of operations they had performed and their batting average. Dr. Damus had the top slugging average (number of operations times the success rate). Actually, that is something I just made up, but the good doctor did have the best figures.

But how to get this man to do the deed? Barbara got to work. She called friends, she called cousins and they called their friends and relatives. One cousin had a good friend whose son was a doctor at St. Francis and he arranged for Dr. Damus to take my case. Now all I needed was a bed in St. Francis. For a week I waited in Huntington

Hospital hooked up to an IV drip, keeping me loaded with blood thinner, and wearing an electronic heart monitor that would sound an alarm if my heart started to fail. Oh joy!

New Year's Eve was celebrated with one other patient and two nurses' aides drinking grape juice (a poor substitute for wine) and eating cookies. A few friends were at my home and I called to wish them Happy New Year (I really was not very happy, though).

Eventually I was ambulanced to St. Francis and my catheterization pictures reviewed by the balloon doctors (they get the first crack at artery fixing). They essentially said, "No can do" - too many blockages. That is what Dr. Gurian had predicted.

The plumber goes to work

There is an expression in the old cowboy movies where doctors are referred to as "sawbones". Now I really know why. Dr. Damus was going to saw my bones, namely my breastbone to get at my clogged pipes. (When he talked to me for the first time, the night before the operation, he said he was just a "glorified plumber". Too bad there's not the medical equivalent of Draino.) It seems I needed a combination carpenter and plumber.

All I remember before the operation was being given a sedative. My next memory as I slowly returned to consciousness was that of gagging on the respirator tube shoved down my throat. During the three-hour interim, there were some very skilled surgeons carving me up and then putting me back together. First, a three-foot long vein was removed from my left leg. Then my breastbone was sawed open and my vitals connected to a heart-lung machine. (This allowed me to stay alive while my heart was somewhere else – like outside my chest.) The vein was cut into several pieces and sewn onto the heart arteries to enable the blood to flow unimpeded when everything was reconnected. All parts were then carefully placed into my chest cavity and my breastbone closed up with a few stainless steel stitches. A few hours later I was sitting in the ICU with a garden hose (drain) sticking out of my stomach. It was a successful quadruple bypass, sometimes called a coronary artery bypass graft or CABG (pronounced cabbage).

Recovering

The next day I tried to walk ten minutes every hour. It was a struggle, I felt like hell, but I had been told that exercise speeds the recovery. I was not told that too much exercise impedes the recovery. And that is what happened. I felt so bad, it took an extra day to recover well enough to go home. Eventually, after eight days I left St. Francis and continued my recovery at home. It was late January 1994 and for the next six weeks I sat (and walked in circles) around the house trying to straighten out my left leg that had this huge ankle-to-groin wound that did not seem to be healing (it was and it did). Also, I had chest pains requiring an overnight stay in the hospital (including another angiogram that proved negative), it snowed every few days (neighbors were kind enough to keep clearing it away), the house was cold, and in general I was feeling very sorry for myself. Barbara was extremely tolerant, listening to my complaints, and coming home from work at noon every day to make me lunch. It seems that most of my problems were mental and I was back to work full time in March and up at the Sperry Ski Lodge for a weekend of skiing in April.

The years since have been good with no limitations on any physical activities. I did have occasional anxiety attacks worrying about my heart and arteries for the first few years after the operation, but all subsequent tests have always proved negative.

Three cheers for modern medicine!

LAUNCHING OF THE SEA HAG

Ship ahoy

It was May 19, 2001 when the Sea Hag made its inaugural launching in Huntington Harbor, Huntington, New York. A description of that launching along with a little background follows:

My son Joseph is in his thirties, single and shares a rented house with his sister, Bobbi, and his good friend Kyle Roberts. He works three or four days a week repairing musical instruments and another two or three days building electric violins. (What? You've never heard of an electric violin?) Actually neither had I, but apparently there is a thriving market for this instrument that is a hybrid of an electric guitar and a violin. Shaped like a space age guitar, but without frets and played with a bow, it is the avant-garde instrument of many popular rock groups including Cyndi Lauper's band. As you might guess, Joseph (that is what his mother and I always call him) marches to a different drummer or should I say dances to a different fiddle. He has long hair (Joseph would you at least put it in a ponytail?) doesn't like to dress up – don't think he ever learned to tie a necktie – but has loads of friends, and always has a smile on his face as he goes through life doing his own thing.

The boat

Joseph has a habit of being very single minded. If he sets a goal of getting something, that something becomes permanently imbedded in the gray matter in his head. Once it was a black electric guitar that his mom and I said was too expensive. Another time it was a Subaru Brat (that is a car not an ornery kid). We did not stand a chance, he got them both.

Now it was a sailboat. I thought it was a great idea – at first. Naturally if you're going to buy a boat and you don't know the first thing about sailing you start off with a small boat. You buy a small boat that can be trailered from your driveway to a local boat-launching ramp. You buy a small boat with a centerboard that will swing up if run into shallow water because you don't know how to sail that well, or are not familiar with the water depth. You buy a small boat that is easy to learn to sail and maneuver, a small boat that is easy to rig as rigging gets quite complex on larger boats.

With that in mind I started to talk to friends who had boats, searched the internet for boating information and in general provided Joseph with all sorts of useful advice to help him make an informed decision on what small sailboat to purchase. (How foolish of me - I had forgotten the black guitar and the Brat.)

Then one night I got the phone call.

"Pop, I bought a 26 foot O'Day sailboat". Now that might not sound big, but it is. Out of the water the hull is much higher than the biggest SUV you ever saw. The mast when attached (and nobody had the vaguest idea how to attach it) would rise an additional 30 feet – that is higher than the peak of my two story house. At 3,500 pounds, with a partial keel and drawing four feet of water with the steel centerboard up, this was not a boat you trailered from the house any time you had a few hours to go sailing. This boat required a heavy-duty truck, special trailer and 200 dollars every time it was to be moved – which meant it was to be moved once to Joseph's house when he bought it and once more to the water at the start of boating season.

It had to be registered and insured, and a mooring had to be rented from a marina. And since the boat was 30 years old there was much work to be done.

Joseph spent the winter and spring refinishing most of the handrails, the bulkheads, the tiller, the rudder. He installed a toilet and new sinks along with the plumbing, rewired the old and corroded electrical system, repaired the transom, installed a motor mount for the ten horsepower outboard and got the motor checked out. And on and on and on.

What is the difference between port and starboard?

There was also another slight problem – how do you sail one of these monsters. The boat when fully rigged (and who knew how to rig it?) would carry hundreds of square feet of sail generating tremendous power, and just how do you go about controlling it? Hanging from the mast that lay on the deck were ropes, cables, shackles, turnbuckles and pulleys. On deck were winches, cleats, shroud attachments and a mast mounting plate. In the cabin were more rope and other hardware associated with the outhaul, downhaul and boom vang (don't ask). All of which were used to rig and sail this beast.

The extent of Joseph's experience were a few Town of Huntington sailing lessons on a twelve-foot dingy when he was ten years old. He had not been in a sailboat since. When I suggested the two of us take lessons at an Oyster Bay sailing school, on a 23-foot Sonar, he agreed. It was a three-day course with most of the time on the water, with just three students and one instructor. We learned about the proper way to sail; we rigged, raised and trimmed sails; sailed in various directions with respect to the wind; reefed the sail for high winds; completed man overboard drills; and learned how to approach a mooring. It was a brief but thorough course on the basics of sailing and Joseph finished up with the confidence that he could certainly handle his boat.

The launching

Then came launch day, with a truck scheduled to take his boat to the water. Joseph had been working frantically to finish as much as possible. A new sink faucet was installed, the motor bracket was mounted, the ladder was attached to the transom (without the bolts being secured – but more about that later). The truck arrived a half-hour early, but where were Joey's friends that he needed to help him? His old man, with a bad back, could only offer moral support – what he needed was physical support. Kyle Roberts and Jim Bowden soon appeared, but new problems would soon arise.

Truck, trailer, boat, Joseph and friends all went to the Huntington Town dock where everything went smoothly - at least for the first twenty minutes. The boat easily floated off the trailer and was secured to the dock. Next step was to mount the outboard on the new bracket. However, Murphy's Law kicked in about this time and when the motor was attached to the bracket the propeller did not reach the water. After a few choice epithets (actually he was just warming up) Joseph drove home to get the necessary tools to reposition the motor mount. With that work completed, the next job was to step the mast. Mounting the mast, called stepping, would proceed with the much-needed help of Jimmy Hahn, who should have been there by now. (Jim was an experienced sailor who had his own boat and had done crewing in some heavy-duty races, like the ocean race from Newport, Rhode Island to Bermuda.) But where was Jim?

Joseph called from his cell phone and left messages. "Jim, I'm having trouble down here at the town dock. Please come and give me a hand as you promised". Each successive call was more frantic and the expletives between calls more salty, to coin a nautical phrase. In the meantime, other boats were being launched and we were tying up dock space. Still, there was no Jim. So when all else fails, what do you do? Read the instructions! That is what we did and the mast went up in a breeze. But - and there's always a but - one of the cable attachments that hold the mast upright was broken and none of the extra hardware on board would remedy the situation. Joe walked to a nearby marine hardware store and returned with another turnbuckle but it was the wrong one. "*%^&$#@*^&%$". Another trip and this time it worked.

Now, one of the mast cables appeared too loose. Jimmy Hahn would know what to do, but where was he? Curses. So they dropped the mast (these neophyte sailors were getting pretty good at this by now) and managed to make an adjustment that resolved the problem. Up with the mast again. Check all the cables – there are six of them holding the mast erect - start the engine, climb aboard and set sail. Not really, there were no sails on board and it was still a little premature to think about actually using wind force for motive power. But the boat was motored out to Huntington Harbor and then back to its mooring at which time the stern ladder, not being firmly secured to the transom dropped into 10 feet of water.

Joseph had followed in his father's footsteps. It had been a bit of a stumble but eventually a successful day. Aside from the ladder.

Post Script

Later that day Jimmy Hahn called. He had been crewing that morning and could not get ashore in time (schedules are tough to keep when onboard a sailboat). He was there the next day to "tune" the rigging.

Within a few days the sails were set and we took it for a sail. It was a bit of a struggle remembering what to do and what order to do it in, but we managed. That summer Joseph went sailing a few times each week (Fridays were reserved for me) and by the end of the season he could rig and unrig the boat in a matter of minutes. He could handle the boat in moderate winds and was becoming familiar with basic navigation. There is a lot to learn in sailing a boat this size and I must say that Joseph was fast becoming a very competent skipper.

MY BIG FAT LONG ISLAND WEDDING

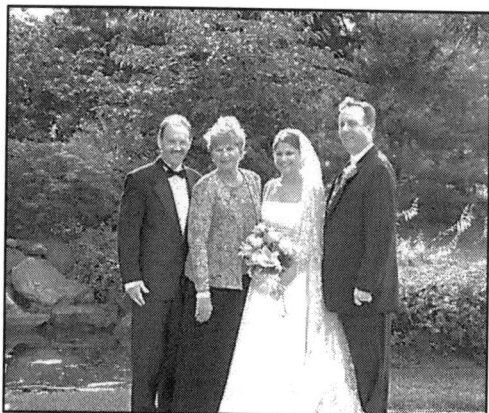

Eloping is not bad either.

"**M**y Big Fat Greek Wedding" is a currently (2002) popular movie about the ethnic problems associated with a mixed marriage. My Big Fat Long Island Wedding is about the wedding of my daughter Bobbi and the trials, tribulations and costs – especially the costs – of a wedding on this well-known island of Long. For starters, this affluent New York City suburb has developed the most decadent life styles known to the free world.

It wasn't always that way. Growing up on LI in the 1930s and 40s in a middle class suburb, us kids in the neighborhood played on the streets and vacant lots nearby. Stickball, punchball, stoopball, handball (Chinese and otherwise), ringalevio, Johnny-Ride-A-Pony, I-Declare-War, and kick-the-can were games requiring little organization (other than sometimes choosing up sides) and a minimum of equipment. No teams, no uniforms, no statistics, no play dates. Birthday parties were usually just with the family and although some of us had parties as we got older (eight or nine) we played simple games like pin-the-tale-on-the-donkey, and had some cake and ice cream. There were relatively inexpensive gifts for the host and no presents for the attendees to take home.

No more. Little kids nowadays are playing Little League baseball and organized soccer with uniforms that include cleated sport shoes and warm up jackets. They are transported from one home to the other for play dates, and birthday parties are annual events more suitable for the heir-apparent to a royal throne than a little kid from the 'burbs. But I digress.

August, 2002

Bobbi will be getting married to Jay Wyman next July, and she and her mother are making plans. I have heard of the outrageous costs associated with Long Island weddings, but only as an innocent bystander. Now it is beginning to sink in - for every person invited to the wedding it will cost me personally after taxes, with no tax write off, about $150. That is a lot of money, especially if there are going to be some 150 guests.

Then there is the question of music. My wife, Barbara, and I were recently at a wedding where the music was so loud that our chests reverberated with the sound, and conversation was absolutely impossible. The young dancers - with their damaged eardrums resulting from years of listening to deafening rock music - were ecstatic, boogying to the raucous rock beat. As a result, a recent conversation between Barbara and Bobbi went like this.

"The older folks – our friends – don't want to listen to that loud music all night"

"But my friends like it."

"Well we're paying for the wedding."

"Then I'll pay for the band."

"Don't you understand, we're paying for the wedding. The band is only a few thousand dollars, we're paying for the rest, which is many thousands of dollars. And where's your ring?"

"I'm leaving."

October, 2002

One evening Bobbi and I went to a wedding band audition. This was nine months before the great day. Can you believe that? I did not realize that an industry had been created around big fat Long Island weddings. Guess it is the result of so many young people getting married (some, more than once). Bobbi told me some of the music played was Motown; it sounded to me like mo' noise. But what do I know? Later, when speaking with the bandleader, he said the volume would be turned down if requested, and that was about all I could hope for. (At the recent wedding reception the most enjoyable moments were when the band stopped playing – it was like taking tight ski boots off after a long day on the slopes.)

Now to select the reception hall. First. there is the basic reception cost, so many dollars per person. Then there are the flowers (a grand or so) and the tips (did you know the maître de gets $250? And that is considered a bargain. It could be up to $1000.) Just found out the bridal attendant gets tipped too. Don't know how much - I never even heard of a bridal attendant before this.

How about the wedding dress? That is where we would certainly save money. Barbara's dress had been embalmed in 1963 in anticipation of a possible daughter getting hitched in the distant future (we did not think it would be so distant, though). Well the dress came out of mothballs (actually an heir-loomed hermetically sealed package) and it looks like something right from the Smithsonian. It is stained and yellow with age – a dress Dolly Madison might have worn two hundred years ago. Besides that, it did not fit. Time to look for a new dress.

November, 2002

It is Thanksgiving time and while sitting around Bobbi's dinner table with Lorna and Lorna's fiancé, Marty, the question of "Where's the ring?" comes up, to which Bobbi says, "See, Jay it's not just my parents asking". Barbara and I have to be careful what we say to Bobbi. Meanwhile the search for a wedding dress continues with trips to bridal salons the length and breadth of Long Island (at least it seems that way).

A reception hall has been selected – the Stonebridge Country Club in Hauppauge. We only have to guarantee 100 people but the list seems to be getting longer all the time. It is well over 150 and I keep thinking of additional people to ask. Coworkers? Friends from Rosedale?

December, 2002

It is now the week before Christmas and still no ring. Then one night, just after Barbara leaves for the store, there is a knock at the door. It is Jay. "Can we talk?" He asks me about marrying Bobbi and wants to show me something. It's "the Ring". And it sure looks sparkling in its Tiffany platinum setting. He will be giving it to Bobbi later this evening. Then they will come back to the house and surprise Barbara, and I will take a picture of the great event. However, later when Bobbi bursts into the house bubbling over with excitement and shows her mom the ring I do not have time to record the event. But it's official. Hallelujah! We can now make the next payment on the wedding reception.

January, 2003

Barbara and Bobbi are still looking for the perfect wedding dress. Even Brandi joins them. All they do is argue. Barbara is always saying "Don't yell at me Bobbi, you asked me to help you pick out the dress". Well the dress was finally selected (nobody asked me anything, except if there was money in the checking account). Next were the bridesmaids' dresses. No matter what Bobbi selects she thinks that at least one of the girls won't like it. She says, "Some of the girls are flat chested and others are bosomy. I don't think Lorna wants a strapless. I don't think Kathy will like the color. Carolyn may not like the style. Mom, why do you look at me that way? Why don't you ever agree with me? Boo hoo."

You know what I would say? Tough. But nobody asks me.

March, 2003

Time marches on. Barbara and I have met Jay's parents on a couple of occasions at Bobbi's condo and they are very nice. This is an unusual situation – only one set of parents for the bride and groom. At recent weddings we have attended, there are usually a variety of stepparents, stepsiblings and half-siblings along with a smattering of full-blooded relatives.

Invitations have been printed, after much arguing over whether I should be Ralph, my birth name, which Barbara insists on, or William, that Bobbi wants and whom everybody but the IRS knows me as. Mom had her way – Ralph it is. As directions are to be included, Jay and Bobbi rode from the church to the reception to the Hampton Inn (hotel for out-of-town guests), clocking mileage and then writing and rewriting the directions.

Barbara and I added to the confusion by providing numerous comments. Speaking of directions, I was directed to provide a map – which I did - but there was no North arrow on it. There was another argument between mother and daughter over that. Mom won out again. The North arrow is there. Mom 2, Bobbi 0.

The latest count is for 210 invitations to be mailed (I think three of them will go to my friends.) The other bad news is that the stock market is still going down.

Meanwhile I have been learning all the words to the Unicorn song that I plan to sing along with Will and Ray at the reception. However all they plan to sing is "Here comes the bride, big fat and wide..." along with making bathroom sounds as they walk down the aisle as ring bearers.

Recently Brandi had a shower for Bobbi at Stephen and Pamela's home. The theme, written on the cake was, "It's about time". I wonder what that meant.

The invitations are returning with about a 99 percent acceptance rate. Doesn't anybody have anything else to do?

June, 2003

It is only a few weeks before the wedding (W-day minus 37 and counting). Bobbi called tonight, in tears, to inform us that her $300 comb (yes that is the right number of zeros) does not fit properly. Barbara will go over to the bridal shop to give them a "what for" and straighten them out. I asked if this comb was really a tiara of some kind, but was told it was a comb. Yes a comb! I would prefer not to even know about things like this. I should be the one who is crying.

W-day minus 7

It is now one week before the big day. Joseph and I were fitted for our tuxedos, but Barbara says my jacket should be a 37 short, not the 38 regular I was fitted for. Also, Jay says my tux should be different from those in the wedding party. So back to Tuxedos Unlimited, or whatever their name is.

Bobbi was over today to make table arrangements (looks like we are down to about 156 people – too bad everyone could not make it). Also, she almost had a meltdown when told – via a phone call from the church - that rose petals could not be used to shower the bride and groom (they represent a slipping hazard). So Barbara is off to buy little bubble pipes for everybody.

Did I mention that Joseph is being evicted and has his heart set on buying a house? The particular house in mind is what is called a "handyman's special", a real handyman's special if you get my drift. Something else to think about amidst all the other preparations.

W-day minus 2

I picked up my tux this morning and must say I look pretty sharp for an old geezer. There is an old saying "clothes make the old man" or something to that effect.

Table arrangements have been agonized over (now the seating tags must be hand written), floral decorations will be delivered Saturday, Joseph has been convinced to break in his new shoes (while he is contemplating the cost of a new cesspool for his possible new home).

The weather has been absolutely horrible so far this spring and summer. The banquet arranger at the Stonebridge Country Club told us today that weather has prevented use of the outdoor patio so far this season. However, the Saturday forecast is for a sunny, warm day. Sure hope so.

W-day plus 1

.....Well. It is all over. The big fat Long Island wedding went off without a hitch. The festivities started Friday evening with a dinner following the rehearsal, hosted by the Wymans at the Inn On The Harbor in Cold Spring Harbor. The next day, at St. Francis Church, Will and Raymond were ring bearers, par excellance, offering no obscene sounds or wise-guy lyrics as they walked down the aisle.

The weather was perfect and our cocktail hour was held on the beautiful Stonebridge outdoor patio. Will, ever the gourmet, announced that the man with the tray had excellent food just for the taking. (At 10 PM when the other kids were sleeping at the table, Will woke up long enough to have desert.)

Jay wanted a picture of himself and Bobbi in one of the Stonebridge golf carts, and after that Lorna's husband Marty hopped in the cart and invited Will, Raymond and their cousin, Stephen Downhower to go for a ride. And go for a ride they did. Marty was reprimanded by one of the staff and told never to drive one again. Marty thought that was funny. Marty thinks almost everything is funny.

Many of Bobbi's associates from her school were there, and Julie (Bobbi's boss) and I, kidded Bobbi about the promotions she keeps refusing. (Someday Bobbi will be a school principal or district superintendent despite all her protests.)

The music was loud by my standards (I twice told the band to tone it down to the level of a roaring subway train) but the young (under 50 crowd) had a great time dancing to the nine-piece band.

The Domjan and Blatnicky grandkids had a wild time dancing, eating and then playing under the tables, but by 10 PM they were all sound asleep and had to be carried to their cars.

The wedding is now behind us and Bobbi and Jay are honeymooning in France and Italy. Our world has returned to normal. The wedding was a great success and if we choose to relive it there are about a thousand pictures (amateur and professional) and a half dozen videos that can be endlessly viewed.

Joseph, Bobbi and Stephen

21 RIDGE ROAD

It is where four generations of the Blatnicky-Domjan family have lived.

The year was 1952. I was a high school dropout serving my second year in the U.S. Army stationed at Ft. Benning, Georgia. The country was in the middle of the Korean War (or police action as it was called) and Barbara, "Aunt Bob" and Leo, "Uncle Leo" Blatnicky were living in a row-house in Jackson Heights, New York with their two children, Barbara and Paul. Although, the kids had been going to Catholic school, they were getting older now (young Barbara was 16, Paul 13) and their parents were concerned about how the city environment would affect them. Uncle Leo was working at the Sperry Gyroscope Company in Great Neck and Aunt Bob was a stay-at-home mom (that was the common arrangement in those by-gone days). A move from the city to the 'burbs entailed a search of Long Island.

The move to Long Island

Aunt Bob's brother Bill and sister Mae each had summer homes in Centerport (known as Huntington Beach in those days) and being familiar with the area, that was where they first looked. In nearby Cold Spring Harbor, some fellow Sperry workers were building homes and when visiting the site they saw other homes built for speculation by a local builder, George Hahn (who was also a Town of Huntington judge). Most had been sold but there were three left on Ridge Road. Leo and Bob decided on the house they wanted, prepared to buy it and then at the last moment Aunt Bob got cold feet. It was too far away from family and friends in the Jackson Heights area and besides she did not have a driver's license (she had just recently failed the test) and a car was the only way to get around on Long Island. However, later that year she had a mind change (a woman's privilege) and a final decision was made to buy the 21 Ridge Road home. Except it really was not 21 Ridge Road, as it did not have a numbered address. There was no mail delivery in the area and mail was picked up at the post office. Letters were addressed to the Blatnickys at PO Box 685, Cold Spring Harbor, NY.

Telephone operators in Huntington Village at the corner of Woodbury and Main would say "Number please" when you picked up the phone, and somebody calling the Blatnickys would ask for Cold Spring Harbor 2-8536. Later the number was changed to MYrtle 2-7212, and calls were dialed via a rotary ring on the phone (still no pushbuttons, area codes or annoying answering machines).

Once settled on Ridge Road it was important for Aunt Bob to get a driver's license. Even more important was to learn to drive. Although getting around in Jackson Heights without a car was no problem (they did have a 1948 Hudson that Uncle Leo drove), there was very little in the way of public transportation on Long Island. After a couple of tries she managed to pass the test (Uncle Leo claims he paid off the inspector). The car that I remember Aunt Bob having when I first met Barbara was a salmon colored 1954 Plymouth station wagon. (That color was referred to as "nipple pink" by Aunt Bob's brother Ed).

Life in Cold Spring Harbor

Barbara was in The Mary Louis Academy at the time of the move and continued to make the trek into Jamaica each day for the next year and a half. Paul transferred to the local Catholic grammar school, St.

Patrick's where he graduated in 1953 and then went to Chaminade High School, a top rated parochial school in Mineola, Long Island. Uncle Leo made his daily commute into Great Neck each morning. At home he held court with the various relatives providing sage advice to all comers. He was "The Godfather". He became an active member of the Lions, was treasurer of the local public library and played cards regularly with some of the neighbors. Aunt Bob was busy worrying about the kids, preparing excellent meals and playing bridge. She also had three sisters, three brothers and many nieces and nephews to keep up with.

There were very not many homes in the neighborhood in the early 50s – there was no Heritage Court and very few homes on Ridge Road, which only ran the short distance between Glen Way and Fox Hunt Lane. The half-acre property was a lot of work, especially in the fall when literally hundreds of thousands of leaves had to be raked. (Uncle Leo threatened to move back to NYC each fall.) There were no leaf pickups, so most people burned their leaves, and at that time of year all Long Island had the smoky smell of burning leaves. It was not a bad smell and was part of the changing of the seasons. However, some poison ivy got incinerated along with the leaves one time and Aunt Bob had a temporary bronchial attack from breathing the toxic fumes.

There were (and still are) huge trees on the property and every year or so one would have to be cut down because it died or was precariously leaning over the Blatnicky house, or one of the neighbors. The tree people would cut it into two-foot lengths and Uncle Leo would spend part of his winter splitting them into firewood. (He said that during a cold spell the sap freezes and they became easier to split)

The den now in the house was not part of the original construction. It was designed by Uncle Leo and added to the house around 1960. It was and is the centerpiece of the house with its wood paneling, high cathedral ceiling and expanse of windows. The floor is slate but in recent years has been covered with carpeting to protect the kids when they fall, which is regularly. (As I write this, my son Stephen, his wife Pamela and their two offspring, Will (7) and Raymond (5) are currently living there.) But that is getting ahead of the story.

The War Room

In 1963 when I first met Barbara, we would go away skiing on weekends with the Sperry Ski Club. On returning late Sunday night, I would stay overnight at the house and go directly into work the next morning. Paul was an ensign in the navy then (he had graduated from Rensselaer Polytech in the ROTC program) and I would sleep in his room. This was the time of the Cuban missile crisis with John Kennedy and Nikita Khrushchev literally playing Russian roulette. Paul was on the aircraft carrier USS Saratoga steaming toward Cuba and his parents were understandably worried.

And on the home front there was the War Room. I have never been able to find it in the house but I know it is there. It was in that room that young Barbara and her mom plotted for my unconditional surrender. There were maps and charts and plotting boards, and it was from this room the "Plan" evolved. Steak on Friday for me even though everybody else was eating fish. (Those were the days when even secular calendars showed a fish on every Friday. Guess it was before Vatican II.) They would let me sleep over in Paul's bedroom on those late returns from skiing. Feed me bacon and eggs for breakfast on Monday morning before heading off to work. Gradually reel me in. And it worked. Now if I could only find that room.

Visiting Grandma and grandpa

In 1963 Barbara and I got married, rented Aunt Mae's home in Centerport, and within a year had baby Stephen and moved to our own home in Greenlawn. In three more years we added Joseph and Barbara (Bobbi) to the brood. Only about seven miles from CSH, we visited regularly. Aunt Bob was now grandma and she would prepare the most delicious meals for us. Grandpa was a serious pipe smoker and the house reeked of tobacco. Although the inspector general had recently come out with a report stating that smoking was dangerous to your health, there were no warning labels on cigarette packs, people smoked in airplanes and movie theaters, and nobody paid much attention to the report. So we just accepted the smell as part of their home. When we left for home at night, grandma would always remind us, "Don't forget to give us two rings when you get home". (Oh, we beat the phone company out of so much money that way.)

Grandpa liked to feed the birds and grandma would render the fat leftovers into suet that she left on the platform he made for them. These birds were probably the biggest and fattest on Long Island. However, these were not the only handouts. There were also many freeloading dogs roaming the neighborhood. The most notorious was Tinker a full-size Great Dane that regularly came to the back door where grandpa always had a special treat. When Joseph was less than two years old he would affectionately maul that dog when he came to the door and Tinker, who was considerably bigger than he was, would just eat his snack and ignore him. (If dogs could smile, I am sure that is what he was doing.)

Time marched on, the kids got bigger, but we still returned to 21 Ridge Road, to visit (and to eat those delicious meals that grandma kept cooking). I say 21 Ridge Road as in the 1960s regular mail delivery was introduced into CSH and everybody got an address number.

Changing of the guard

In 1990, Grandpa died and the house was too much for grandma to maintain herself. She moved into a nearby assisted living facility where she lived until succumbing to heart failure in 1992. Barbara and Paul then had to make a decision as to whether to sell the house or rent it. They had heard horror stories about problems with tenants, but the housing market was down at the time, renting would provide a steady income for grandma's living expenses and maybe the market would improve with time.

The first renters (from 1990 to 1994) were a Japanese couple working on temporary U.S. assignment for the Pall Corporation. The lease was with the Pall Corporation and aside from some unauthorized redecorating, they were good tenants. That is until they unexpectedly moved out before the end of the lease and the Pall Corporation tried to renege on the lease agreement. Paul wrote them in no uncertain terms what their financial obligations were and after a few heated discussions and exchanges of letters their corporate attorney backed down and paid what was owed (one of the few times in recorded history that a lawyer got his come-uppance).

Then there was Angela, the modern version of Marlene Deitrich. She was the Berlin bombshell, a divorcee, with many current paramours. She rented from 1994 to 1998.

During this rental period Stephen and Pamela were married (1996) and moved from NYC to an apartment in Port Washington where William was born in 1997. The following year they started to look for a house in the Port Washington area but the homes were much too expensive for what they offered. At about the same time Angela's lease was up and she did not want to renew it, but agreed to stay on a monthly basis. Now Barbara and Paul had to decide what to do – try renting it again or sell it. In talking with a real estate broker to establish a sale price, they were told the market for homes in this area was awful. In fact, the average selling price was going down at a rate of about one percent a month. Stephen and Pamela really did not want to move out further on the island because of his long commute to the city, but the relatively low price of a home in Cold Spring Harbor, plus a little price break on Barbara's half of the house, was sufficient incentive to move into the old homestead.

And so in the summer of 1998 the fourth generation of the same family (William) moved into the house on 21 Ridge Road. Another fourth generation member, Raymond, arrived in December 1999.

There was a brief scare in 2002 when Stephen lost his job and was out of work for almost nine months. For a while it looked like they might have to move if another job did not come through. But it did and the fourth generation of the Blatnicky-Domjan family continues to occupy the old homestead.

THE COURT

In February 2005 Barbara and I moved from the court – Nine Pine Hollow Court to be specific. We had been there 41 years.

Sometimes they're called cul-de-sacs, or dead-end streets, but no matter the name, the court of Pine Hollow offered a special way of living and of bringing up kids. Our home, one of about a hundred in a development called Carriage Hill, was the first home Barbara and I ever bought. We really did not know much about what to look for in a house – we later said the next one we will know exactly what we want. However, there were only three model homes (a small colonial, a larger colonial and a high ranch) and 50 acres of farmland when we placed our down payment with the salesman (the larger colonial, please). He told us – and we believed it – that no two identical models would be built next to each other and they would all be painted different colors. What a joke.

Ninety percent of the homes were the larger colonial with natural cedar shakes on the front and white asbestos shingles on the sides and back. We did not elect to get upgraded windows (the sliders that came with the house were junk) or an extra room for $250, or extra electrical outlets or 200-amp electrical service or any one of a number of extras that seemed unnecessary and overly expensive at the time. However, the one thing we did get was a house on a court with a slightly larger lot, all for the exorbitant price of $23,000.

Children of the court

Stephen was one when we moved in, Joseph was born shortly after and Bobbi two years later. They were children of the court.

There are eleven homes in the court and in 1964 almost all were lived in by young families with children. Chrissie and Karen Muir on the left, Robbie and Diane Sheppis on the right, and Jimmy and Mary Ellen Kiernan across the street. And there were others. Lloyd Spivak lived down the street (he was Stephen's age) and was the resident quiz kid. He knew north from south and even where the Long Island Expressway was. My kids were lucky if they knew the difference between the front and back yards.

Life on the court

The court had no traffic and very few cars even parked in the street. The most cars ever seen there occurred when the Volkswagen Corporation staged an ad with five or six VW bugs being the only vehicles in sight. Ours was included – a 1960 red VW – with Stephen and Joseph (then three and two) sitting in the back seat. The resulting ad was in the 1968 and 1969 Volkswagen brochures distributed by most VW dealers in the country.

Moms in those days were stay-at-home, and the kids were play-at-home. Play dates, summer camp or mindless TV were not required to keep the kids entertained; they had the court. There were bicycles, tricycles, wagons, fire trucks, roller skates, balls, chalk and a variety of other toys to play with. But most of all there were other children to play with, in a safe and secure environment.

As they got older some kids got involved with organized sports; baseball, football and soccer being the most popular. I personally disliked Little League where kids would be spotlighted in the batter's box with the opposing team taunting, "No batter, no batter", then cheering if the poor kid struck out. Way too much pressure on little kids. When my boys were involved I was behind the plate calling balls and strikes. Whenever the call was close, I would be verbally abused by half the parents in the stands. Gordon MacMillan (high school principal, former college athlete, and absolute whiz working with kids) was a manager who played everyone equally, taught the kids the fundamentals of the game and the spirit of good sportsmanship. As a result his teams did not win many games and he was disliked by many Little League parents and officials. *How foolish of him.*

Conversely, the court provided equal access to all the kids regardless of age, sex, size or athletic ability. It was a good place to have a good time.

Moving on

Now our own children have grown and have youngsters of their own. Barbara and I have moved to a nearby condo community and although we miss the court and the kids, it was time to move on and let the next generation move in. Our grandchildren are grand children that visit us regularly at our new townhouse. We take them to the pool, go bike riding and do other things with them– but it is not quite the same as life was, many years ago on Pine Hollow Court.

Post Script

We realized after moving into our new condo that we did not select all the best options for flooring and tiles, and did not get all the extras we could really use. Maybe the next house.

WAR OF THE ROSES

I mistakenly thought I was done with gardening.

I brought with me no gardening tools when in 2005, Barbara and I moved from Greenlawn – our home of 41 years – to our townhouse in The Greens (a gated, guarded, private, upscale condominium community, and fully equipped with hot and cold running immigrants to perform all the landscaping chores). None. No hose, trowel, shovel, rake or gloves. We did not get an outdoor outlet for a hose (it was an extra $500 and just why would I need one?). My green thumb could now gracefully turn old, wrinkled and gray - like the rest of me. But I was wrong.

Our townhouse is one of four units in a single building. There are hundreds of these buildings in The Greens, they all look alike and it suits me fine. I have no desire for individuality, to stand out among the masses. I can still find my way to 521 Bardini Drive without using breadcrumbs. The Home Owner's Association to whom we pay a monthly stipend, maintains the multitude of trees, bushes and flowers outside our homes and throughout The Greens common properties. They do an OK, if not great, job that I can live with, or thought I could until this summer.

Although a few people have enhanced their homes with extra plantings, most have been of my ilk - let the HOA do it. Not so my neighbors. The three other families in this building seem to be in a war of the roses (well - maybe they are black-eyed Susans, or day lilies or zinnias). Visitors complement us on the beautiful flowers under our front bedroom window. However, Alan and Renee (neighbors on the right) planted them next to their front door that is also next to our bedroom window.

There are large earthen berms on either side of our building. Lois and Ellis (neighbors on our left) and Debbie, Frank and Al (neighbors on their left) have covered one with hydrangeas, impatiens, and other flowers, and recently had it covered with a fresh coating of pine bark mulch. Al is out every evening watering it all. Barbara and I made a lame attempt to add some plantings to the other berm (I borrowed Frank's shovel.) The impatiens died immediately, the hydrangeas took a little longer.

Our neighbors continued their horticultural attacks with plantings across the rear of the property. It started on the left with Debbie and Frank's flanking assault of flowers followed by Lois and Ellis's flowers, shrubs and even solar powered border lights. And Renee and Alan initiated a pincer attack with more botanical plantings coming from their side.

Our building was now surrounded by a colorful treat of natural splendor - except for a few barren patches of territory associated with the Domjans. What's a guy to do? Especially since Ellis offered me unlimited use of his hose and Alan offered me his shovel. Alan even offered to help me plant. I had two choices: one – sit outside, relax and stare at the bleak landscape and receive back even bleaker stares from the neighbors; or two – capitulate.

Offering minimal resistance, I yielded to their unspoken but strongly implied demand of unconditional surrender. With my new shovel in hand and following directions from Barbara, I struggled to penetrate the near concrete-like "soil" in the backyard. I eventually dug about ten holes (I should have used explosives) and planted the flowers Barbara had bought. Words cannot describe their beauty.

But that's not the end – now they have to be watered regularly!

NIGHTMARE ON WEST NINETEENTH STREET

A house that required infinite work just to be upgraded to a handy man's special.

Number two son, Joseph, who rented a home in Huntington Station for the last 13 years was notified in the spring of 2003 that the house was being sold. Did he want to buy it? The price was unreasonable and Joe decided to leave. He contacted a real estate agent, lined up another house nearby that was affordable (a handyman's special that is the subject of this little essay) and went to contract. However, red tape and bureaucratic delays prevented him from closing on the "new" house, yet he had to leave the old house almost immediately. What to do? Where to go? What to do with all that "stuff" that accumulated over the years? Boxes and boxes of boxes and boxes.

Back to the nest

Our basement, that was no bargain to begin with, became filled with his stuff. The two-car garage was now a no-car garage. It was an electric violin factory. In it were a table saw, band saw, drill press, compressor, work benches, cabinets, a multitude of hand tools and an extra heavy duty extension cord that wound its way through the garage, out across the patio, into the partially opened kitchen door, through the mud room, across the kitchen floor, and up onto the counter into a twenty amp electrical outlet. It ran across the same kitchen floor that many, many years ago he played on with his Tonka trucks while Barbara was preparing his dinner. Now he played with only one truck, a Toyota and it was parked in the driveway. Barbara was once again preparing his dinner. Joe was a breath of fresh air that reentered our lives. Especially now since the kitchen door did not close all the way.

The nightmare becomes apparent

But I digress. That was September. Come October and there were requests for a termite inspection, title insurance, and mortgage application. Oh, and I forgot to say, in the meantime Joseph had lost his job as a musical instrument repairman (company went out of business) and Barbara and I told him he should collect unemployment. And so he did, but when he mentioned this to his attorney, a former player in Joseph's band, he was told it could seriously jeopardize his getting a mortgage. We all went into a deep funk. Then in mid-October the phone rang – mortgage approved, insurance policy received, walk through in two days with closing the following day. The deed was about to be done.

The walk through (for me it was a stumble through as I had broken my foot the week before) was done with Joseph and Susan, (the real estate agent who was a little bit embarrassed about the transaction – she kept saying what a large piece of property this is, as it was the only redeeming feature). The house was roach infested, windows were broken, the cellar had mold-covered walls, sheet rock hanging from the ceiling and unprotected 120 volt electrical wires loosely twisted together to provide power for the lights. The upstairs walls had holes in them, the floors were badly worn, the doors broken and the house could not be locked. Of course there was no reason to.

The house on West Nineteenth Street was truly a nightmare. No ghosts, goblins, hatchet murderers or witches were there. It was far worse than that. First, imagine a small two-story building built in 1930 on a half-acre of property. Then, Huntington was a relatively small community and there were only a few scattered homes in the neighborhood. Sometime later it was converted to a legal two family home consisting of a tiny apartment on each floor with a separate upstairs entranceway added. Over the years new homes were slowly added to the neighborhood and it became a thriving middleclass community. Sometime in the 1970s the community started to deteriorate with many of the homes used for rental income. The need for housing was dire and there were many immigrants –legal and illegal – anxious to find living quarters. Now imagine that same house in 2003 with little or no maintenance or repair for the last 30 years. However, many changes had been made that provided a significant income for its owners. The basement was subdivided into three bedrooms (how many bodies to a bedroom is unknown), a shed with six built-in bunk beds was added to the two-car garage. And who knows how many people were crammed into the two tiny apartments in the house?

Not only was the house neglected, the yard became a veritable junk yard with refuse including toilet bowls, appliances, bicycles, scooters and old tools littering the property. Did I mention the garage? The house was a palace compared to the garage. That building was ready to fall down as a result of old rotted beams and a gaping hole in the roof (in it was an abandoned car and mountains of junk).

Now for an aside about the cockroaches. Multi-generations of these creatures infested the entire building. Barbara insisted Joseph get an exterminator. He did – himself. Fumigating bombs were set off in each of the six rooms on a number of nights, followed by the setting of high potency professional traps. Barbara became concerned that Joe would bring some insects home (he was still living at home while preparing the House on West Nineteenth Street for habitability) and she had him change his clothes in our garage each time he returned from cockroach heaven. More than once he entered the house in his BVD's.

The big cleanup

Meantime Todd Brummer (a future tenant) was coming in from Glen Cove each afternoon to help clean out the refuse and prepare the inside of the building for a paint job.

With the mountain of trash piled high in the driveway, Joseph rented a 20 cubic yard dumpster for its removal (at a cost of five hundred dollars). Also, Barbara called the Town of Huntington to ask about appliance pickups. They asked for the address and when told said, "Oh yeah, we know about that place. We know you have 11 appliances at the curb. We'll pick them up when we get a chance". Joseph gave them a few dollars when they came by to ease the pain.

Over the next two months Joe, assisted by his friends and especially Todd, cleaned out the garage, cut down most of the overgrown brush, tore out a number of plaster walls, painted the upstairs apartment, cleaned and waterproofed the basement, had the place fumigated, removed old outdated electrical wiring, and in general made the place livable. At the same time Joe was busy hand crafting his electric violins for Mark Wood. He was a busy, busy young man.

The weather that fall had been relatively mild allowing Joseph to continue working on his violins in our garage as well as working on his home. Progress was being made, but there was just so much to do. His friends came over regularly to help.

Additional brush was cut to clear the large yard, the garage rafters and support beams were shored up to prevent the imminent collapse of the roof. A shed that would be used for painting had to be raised at one end by about a foot to make it level. His 26-foot sailboat was brought to the backyard for winter storage, old interior house walls were removed, a stove and refrigerator were purchased, delivered and then squeezed up a narrow staircase for the upstairs kitchen. The old upstairs shower was cut up and thrown out.

The basement, along with everything else in the house had been neglected for years. This was to be the workshop and it had to be thoroughly cleaned, walls and floors prepared for waterproof painting (there had been some leaks noticed during heavy rains) and then painted. Even then, the floor paint started to peel in spots and would require additional work.

At least it was not cold and the old, long neglected oil burner was clunking away providing adequate heat for the small house. However, on December 1, the weather turned significantly colder (below freezing at night) and the oil burner decided it was just too tired to continue operating. Joe called his neighbor, who he had allowed to use his dumpster, who in turn called his friend who would come by in a few hours to look at it. The few hours turned into a day and a half, with Joseph running two kerosene heaters to maintain enough heat to prevent the pipes from freezing. The repairman finally showed up, got the burner running (clogged fuel line) and Joe was back in business, just waiting for the next crisis. It was also getting very cold to work on the violins in our garage, even with the auxiliary heaters.

Leaving the nest

By January 2004 all the heavy equipment had been moved from my garage to Joe's garage. He would no longer freeze at my place. He had his own place to freeze in. This meant more work on the garage and shed to provide a reasonable work environment. The upstairs apartment had new kitchen and bathroom sinks, a refrigerator, stove, toilet and shower. It also had a new rent-paying tenant, Todd Brummer. Joe's basement workshop had been completed also, but his apartment still needed much work. Like a stove, refrigerator, new bathroom, even walls. It was barely habitable, however there were other priorities. These were principally the completion of many electric violins that customers were clamoring for. Pressed by Mark Wood and his need for some cash inflow, Joe started spending most of his time working on the instruments.

....It is now the summer of 2004 and Joe is still busily working on his garage, his home, his instruments and his sailboat. It is a busy life for him and he appears to thoroughly enjoy it.

WORLD TRADE CENTER ATTACK 9/11/01

The following notes were made in the first few weeks after the World Trade Center attack.

Tuesday, September 11, 2001
I had just returned to my part time job with Parsons Brinckerhoff after a three-day weekend at Montauk Point. Rick Knowlden, INFORM Traffic Systems project manager, and I were talking on the phone about some water damage that had occurred at the office and also some relatively minor personnel problems. At the time, the operators at the control center had a commercial TV channel on along with the other monitors displaying traffic conditions on the Long Island roads. At 8:45 AM Rick interrupted our conversation to tell me a plane had crashed into one of the World Trade Center towers, and then had to hang up. I went downstairs to listen to my car radio, thinking this was a singular accident – terrorism did not even enter my mind. Then, it was announced there was another explosion in the South Tower, followed shortly by the fact that it was a second plane crash. There was no mention that these were terrorist attacks and I am not sure just when I realized that was the case.

Shortly after, I drove to the control center closely listening to the radio and then spent most of the day there watching the story unfold on television. There were many conflicting reports, including a helicopter crashing at the Pentagon (it was a commercial airliner) and a plane being shot down over the Potomac River near DC (not true). Most people were amazed at the events but nobody seemed furious, although someone suggested we nuke them (whoever "them" might be).

Somebody from the State office was to go to a meeting at the WTC. Jack Randazzo (a State employee at INFORM) was concerned about his brother-in-law who worked there (he was OK). An e-mail from the PB city office stated that 15 PB employees were working out of the WTC. No word on any of them. I left the control center for home at about 6 PM and called back at 8 PM volunteering to come in if necessary. Not required. INFORM worked closely with police in displaying messages indicating closures on roads into the city (Southern State Parkway, Northern State Parkway and Long Island Expressway). Spent the evening watching TV with constant replays of the collapse of the twin towers. Don't know anybody, as of now, that was lost or even affected by crashes even though expected casualties are in the thousands. The whole event has not sunk in to me yet, although it seems that right now this will be a turning point in the way we live.

Wednesday September 12, 2001

Went to control center at State Office Building in Hauppauge. Two female police officers politely questioning all people entering and asking for ID. Showed driver's license and explained I worked for INFORM. No problem. Later the police left (it is a public building housing the Motor Vehicle Bureau, Workman's Compensation court and other offices the public requires access to). Rick asked me to make up some ID badges for our Parsons Brinckerhoff employees using a program he had downloaded from the internet. Used digital camera to take photos, including my own, digitally inserted them into an authentic looking badge template, typed in the appropriate names, had them signed and then laminated them into very official looking badges. (So much for any difficulty in breaching security.)

Jim Lapine, an INFORM inspector, said that many members of his local volunteer fire department were NYC firefighters and were missing. Still do not personally know anyone directly affected, but obits are starting to include some of the well-known people who died.

Played golf with Wiley League and conversation was pretty much with respect to tragedy. John Sharrer, one of Wiley's young engineers, told me his girlfriend took pictures from her nearby office building and he would send them to me the next day. Had spirited conversation after golf over what to do in response to attacks.

Thursday, September 13, 2001

No work (usually only work Monday through Wednesday). Received pictures from John.

From: "John Sharrer" <jsharrer@wileyengineering.com>
To: <wdomjan@juno.com>
Date: Thu, 13 Sep 2001 08:07:11 -0400
Subject: WTC DISASTER

These are some pictures my girlfriend took from her office and the street when she was leaving her building. Her building is in the foreground of the WTC with the blue tarps on the top.

My daughter-in-law's parents were scheduled to fly to Buffalo on their way home to Canada, but since all flights were cancelled this week, they will now leave next Monday (this was later changed to returning via Amtrak on Saturday). The weather has been beautiful all week, including our weekend in Montauk, and is frequently mentioned in the news reports when contrasting it with the devastation. It seems strange, with most of the cable TV channels and radio stations having continuous coverage of this historical event, my everyday life has not changed, at least not yet. I am curious as to when the infuriating (at least to me) commercials will start to return. One measure of a tragedy is just how long the TV reporting remains commercial free. Another is the size of the headline in the New York Times (the paper of record I annoyingly and frequently tell my wife Barbara). It was not a full banner, like the start of WWII but it probably was similar to the Apollo moon landing in 1969. (Should check on this.)

Friday September 14

Rainy and cool today. I had been looking at the disaster from a distance as if it was an earthquake or typhoon in some far off location, but the tragedy is sinking in more each day. Last night Bobbi told of two young children in her school that lost fathers. Lay in bed thinking about it. Yes, the unimaginable happened. Not much I can do in response. Volunteers not needed (they seem to be screwing up operations in the city) blood banks have more blood than they can use. Will donate $100 to a WTC charity. Checked web to see if my skills, whatever they may be, could be useful. No luck so far. Got a haircut today, and sent my digital camera back for repair. Had tickets to take my grandson to see the Long Island Ducks baseball game this evening but it was cancelled. So was tomorrow's Cow Harbor Race that Frank Springer is coming down from Maine to participate in. Maybe we will go for a bike ride. It will be interesting to hear Frank's take on this.

Rode my exercise bike and caught the last half hour of the memorial service at the Washington National Cathedral (find myself watching more, not less TV). Heard that proselytizing old windbag, the Most Reverend Billy Graham, telling everybody that God would save us. (I feel very strong about this country being the greatest in the world but I do not appreciate Christianity being the only valid religion here.) President Bush gave an impressive speech, but as with any politician, I wonder who wrote it. Lord's Prayer sung by gorgeous black singer (Denise?-opera?) and Battle Hymn of the Republic by uniformed chorus were very emotional. Odd selection as "Battle" was song of the North during the Civil War.

Saturday September 15, 2001

Frank arrived last night around 7 PM. (I called too late to let him know the Cow Harbor Race was cancelled). He ran with informal group of about 50 runners, some carrying flags. Had police escort and all stayed together. Ended in Northport Park with moment of silence followed by runners and spectators saying names of those they knew who died at WTC. Spoke with Brian Asher while waiting for runners. His ideas are typical of most people. Willing to give up some freedoms for better security. Frustrated about lack of particular enemy to strike back at.

More stories of too many volunteers at site and too many supplies. Would like to help and hope that some time in near future I can do so. Stephen is going with his friend Chris Horner to a Red Cross office on the island to provide some assistance. Will check with him if I can help. Feel guilty but do not feel like going to memorial services. Don't believe that will help but would like to provide some material help in addition to donating money.

Went out with Frank this afternoon, met his son Billy at Bethpage Park and painted directional arrows between Bethpage Bikeway and bike path to Jones Beach at Cedar Creek Park (we have gotten very confused trying to follow the old worn out arrows. Lots of kidding around about "crime" being committed, but major benefit to biking community. Frank said if I am jailed he will spend next 20 years, if necessary, to get me freed. Stephen, Pamela and boys over for dinner. "New" castle Barbara and Bobbi bought at garage sale a big hit with kids. Biking and family visit was pleasant break of generally unpleasant atmosphere pervading country.

Monday September 17

Back to work today. Stock market opens today. Wonder what the results will be. Noticed that TV channels are getting back to normal with scheduled programs being aired along with commercials. Went to Stephen's last night for dinner. Boys don't appear to have any significant knowledge of event. Novak and Jo Ann (Pamela's free spirited friends) were near WTC at time of attack and saw whole thing. They ran uptown to Penn Station got on LIRR and then were evacuated 40 minutes later. Scared.

Warehouse space needed for excess of supplies being received (tons of dog food has been received for the few K-nine sniffers being used). Jim Lapine said two of his police officer brothers are busy photographing and fingerprinting body parts brought into temporary morgues. Still would like to find way to help. Will look for something worthwhile. Probably send more money at minimum. A little concerned about Stephen's outlook for a job (job market was not very good before WTC attack).

Sent the following email to the NY Times

I probably speak for many when I ask what can I do to help out in this emergency? Food, blood and other items seem to have been contributed in abundance and volunteers are not wanted at the site. Although memorial services, lighting candles, setting up makeshift shrines and displaying the flag provide some spiritual relief, many of us want to do something material, something specific rather than just watching the results of this horrible devastation. Sending money has been done. Now what can we do?

Bill Domjan

Greenlawn, NY

Market down almost 700 points. Started noticing more commercials on CNN.

Sunday September 23, 2001

It has been a few days since my last entry. The major news remains stories of the WTC disaster. Bush gave his best speech ever before Congress last Thursday night. Most, but not all conversations include comments about the attacks. Went to Ed and Pat Babor's 25th wedding anniversary party yesterday where many of the cousin's generation (born 1930s and thereabouts) attended. Frankie Babor (about 80 years old) was the only WWII veteran cousin attending. He was a B-24 pilot (did not see action). Paul and Carol Blatnicky flew in from Cleveland and said airport parking lots, terminals and planes were sparsely populated. Many police at MacArthur Airport curbside drop-off and pickup, and they did not allow any waiting at curb. There is much concern about possible recession (economy was slowing down before attack) and Dow Jones down 1300 points (14%) this week. Have not checked my portfolio of mutual funds and will probably wait for my monthly statement. Business down at NYC hotels, restaurants and Broadway shows. This will pick up with time if there are no further terrorist attacks. My concern is that a suicide bomber will blow himself up in the middle of crowded Times Square or in a subway. That would really destroy morale, which is only very slowly improving.

Thursday October 11, 2001

It has been a month since the attack on the WTC and there has been no letup in the papers, TV or radio. Almost all the news is devoted to the event. Last Sunday we started bombing Afghanistan and Bin Laden stated they would retaliate and no American was safe. Life goes on (I played golf last night) but everybody is on edge. Today President Bush was on TV warning about possible terrorist attacks in the next few days. Pamela is working in the city next week and wants Stephen to stay with her because she is afraid. Stock market has been rebounding somewhat but I do not closely watch my portfolio, just look at my monthly statements. Really don't know what is going to happen next.

October 22, 2001

It has been over a month since the WTC disaster and it is still the major subject of the news. We started an air assault in Afghanistan along with some commando raids two weeks ago and although in general we have Muslim support there are many protests among them around the world. Also, anthrax has been discovered in a number of places in the U.S. with one person dying from it. The cable news networks have 24-hour coverage and they pretty much say the same thing as each other and also continually repeat the same news themselves. They all have retired generals, admirals, ex commandos etc. providing their interpretation of the news. Although this is serious business, the Gary Condit missing aide story (with sexual implications) was given the same coverage before September 11. Ditto for O. J. Simpson and the Clinton scandals.

I watched a TV special from Madison Square Garden Saturday night and saw one of the NYC firemen from my RAGBRAI bike rides in Iowa be introduced by Mayor Giuliani and make the statement, "I'm from Far Rockaway and Osama bin Laden can kiss my royal Irish ass. He killed my brother John". I had spoken to John on my 1998 Iowa bike ride and Frank Springer took a picture of us talking together. RAGBRAI website had article from Des Moines Register about Mike, John and the NYC firefighters.

I sent the following email:

From: wdomjan@juno.com

To: tammypav@aol.com,pete@pkbelly.com

Date: Fri, 26 Oct 2001 10:25:38 -0400

Subject: NYC Firefighter

Tammy/Pete,

Sorry I did not make RAGBRAI the last two years but maybe next year (maybe even Frank). Attached is an article and picture that appeared in Newsday last week about Mike Moran. The photo is with his cousin Joe Crowley who also rode with Pork Belly. Thought you might be interested. There was also another interesting article in the Register about Mike and the rest of the NYC firefighters that you most probably have seen on the RAGBRAI website (I have included that also). Hope everything is going well with you folks and your families.

Bill

October 31, 2001

Halloween. The kids were out in force tonight and things appeared normal. But the news is grim. More anthrax discovered and a fourth person died of it today. Not related to post office and considerable concern of its origin. Not making very much headway in Afghanistan, although US efforts are mainly bombing. Ground action for US troops predicted and surveys indicate U.S. people support this type action.

Tuesday November 13, 2001

It has been 9 weeks since the WTC attack and it is still the major news item each day. The NY Times has a separate section each day devoted only to the war on terrorism. Bush gets high praise from everyone for his leadership but he still is not an impressive speaker without a teleprompter. Last week Barbara flew to Florida (into hurricane Michelle) for a five-day cruise. Heavy security with long waits but she had a good time. Then yesterday a plane leaving JFK crashed in Rockaway, Queens killing 260 people. A day later authorities say it was an accident and not an act of terrorism, but there are many questions to be answered especially in the way the plane fell apart before crashing.

Stephen went for job interview in city today but it did not go well (job/experience mismatch and Stephen over qualified for position).

WAITING FOR THOSE ENDORPHINS

My DNA must be different from other runners.

I started jogging many years ago - it was the early seventies and running was all the craze. Read many books and magazines on the subject, all extolling the virtues of this new activity (ironically, Jim Fixx, the running guru of the time later had a fatal heart attack while participating in his money making exercise). Many articles mentioned something called "the runners high". Supposedly, after running for a while the brain starts to generate substances called endorphins. These act like hallucinogenic drugs making a person feel euphoric as they run. Sounded great.

I ran lunchtime, after work and on weekends. I entered races as short as three miles and as long as 26 miles (the Long Island Marathon – one time). I ran so much my Achilles tendons wore out. Never once did I experience that runner's high. However, I did experience more pain and exhaustion the longer or faster I ran. Kind of what you might expect if you had not read all those running books.

Over the years I have been jogging off and on, the limiting factor being my Achilles tendons that ache and burn when over used. Nevertheless, I still do it occasionally and the other day after jogging about two minutes my legs started to ache and I was getting out of breath. After 30 minutes my legs felt like lead, my lungs were burning and my quadruple bypassed heart was about to leap out of my chest. But you know what? After all these years and all those miles, my 72-year-old brain was still waiting for those endorphins to kick in.

ICE SKATING

It is not like riding a bicycle. You do forget how to do it.

The last time I had skated, with the exception of doing it a few times with my kids when they were young, was almost 60 years ago. The place was on a pond in Brookville Park in Rosedale, NY. It was long before anybody even thought of global warming and winters were usually cold enough to freeze any fresh water ponds or lakes. Except for the six team National Hockey League there was not much need for indoor skating on artificially frozen ice. (There were regular ice boat races on Lake Ronkonkoma and even sometimes on the salty Great South Bay.)

Skating outdoors in the 1950s

It was only a short walk from my house to the pond where I would put on my secondhand pair of hockey skates and then lace them so tight my ankles ached. Those same ankles would then bend nearly down to the ice. I bought ankle supports, laced the skates even tighter, but still no luck. However, I was able to skate, even backwards, making what I thought were pretty neat figure eight turns. Cracking the whip was a favorite activity, where a line of skaters would hold hands and then start skating as fast as they could. When the leader would quickly stop and "crack" the whip, the last couple of skaters would usually not be able to hang on and would go flying head over heels down the pond colliding with whatever happened to be in their trajectory. We never played hockey, never were concerned with technique, never sharpened the blades and never even thought of skating as a sport. It was just something we did in the winter when there was ice on the pond.

Aside: There really was not much monitoring of the ice in those days and one winter, when the pond was frozen, but not too thick, my eight-year-old sister Marge fell through the thin ice. A neighbor looking from his window across the street saw what had happened and was able to rescue her.

Fast-forward six decades.

Bud Mackenzie, an old friend I have known since college, said, "Bill, why don't you go ice skating with me." It was the last thing I was thinking of and said, "Sorry Bud, but I don't have skates." He said, "I have an extra pair I'll lend you." I thought what the heck, I had skated before and like bike riding it was probably something you don't forget. I said, "OK."

I met Bud at his home one Friday morning where he showed me in infinite detail the skate sharpening rituals to be followed when speed skating with him. (I say speed skating because these low profile slick skates have blades about two feet long - only a slight exaggeration - and are designed to move out.) First, the skates get locked into a special jig in preparation for exactly 120 strokes made with a sharpening stone. "Make an oval motion Bill, not just back and forth". Then a second stone is used to hone the blades to razor sharp condition. (These skates would never be allowed as carry-on luggage aboard an airplane.) This is performed every third time the skates are used. I could see that sharpening time would approach ice time.

The gang

Now to the rink. Cantiague Park is a Nassau County Park that includes a large indoor skating rink open to speed skaters for two-hour sessions, three times each week. I expected to see a rink full of skaters of various ages and sexes. However, the rink had not opened yet, and standing around were ten old men. I thought at first they were senior citizens that came to the arena expecting to watch a hockey game. Wrinkled faces, white hair - if they had any. But soon they were lacing up their skates, ready to rock and roll. And that they did. Every one of them was soon effortlessly cruising around the rink, chatting with each other with hands neatly tucked behind their backs. Long smooth powerful strides, gracefully propelled them on the smooth slick ice that had been recently polished by the rink's Zamboni.

After lacing my skates and then standing I fully expected my ankles to go into their old pretzel routine. But no, they remained stiff and upright in the skate boot - I would now be able to show my stuff. I strode across the rubber-tiled floor to the ice, confidently stepped out onto it - and nearly fell on my head. Wow, it is not like riding a bike. This is new and different and I would have to learn all over again. And that is what I tried to do.

About my skating. Where should I begin? That first day I was pretty wobbly and did fall one time. As a kid I fell many times and never thought twice about getting hurt. As an adult after that first session I wore wrist and elbow guards. I am probably considered a sissy, as I am the only one with protective gear except for Norm who wears a helmet. The next session I fell a couple of times but the protective gear did its job and I felt more confident skating. However, at another session I crashed into the wall trying to improve my turning ability, which is close to nil. (Earlier I had to take little baby steps going around the rink in a race that Fred had organized.) I thought some ribs were cracked. I was afraid - not of the injury itself, but how I would explain it to Barbara since we were going on a cruise in two weeks.

Now let me tell you something about these gentlemen I skate with. First of all, I don't understand the mystical attraction they all have for speed skates. Bud drove to Vermont one day a couple of years ago to buy speed skates. With 8 to 10 million people living in our metropolitan area you would think somebody had a shop that sold

156

speed skates. But no, he had to travel 500 miles up and back for these special ones. Then this year he went upstate to Lake Placid – another 500 mile round trip - to buy an even better pair of skates.

To illustrate their dedication – some might say fanaticism – to the sport, Bud and Oovie talk about going to Lake George this winter to take part in a 10-kilometer race on the lake. They talk about it in reverential terms, like Muslims going to Mecca.

It is practically a cult. Speed skates, as the name implies, are for racing – not for hockey, not for figure skating, not for recreational skating. They are made for going straight and fast with an occasional left turn – never right - on an oval track. But I digress. Back to my fellow skaters.

Murray is 80 years old with an arthritic back. Norm, once an expert, now hobbles around the rink. He wears a helmet and may be recovering from an injury or just suffering the ravages of advancing years. Fred – a smooth skater, long and tall with thick white hair is also an avid bike rider. He looks and moves like an athlete but is getting long in the tooth like the rest of the gang. One elderly old codger – can't think of his name - worked on one of the Moran tugboats in New York Harbor and still continuously talks about his experiences. I once overheard him talk about his most famous hero of WWII. He was skipper of a tug at some battle-torn port in Europe. Bill who has hair like Albert Einstein joined us recently. He is just starting to skate again after a 23-year layoff and went to Lake Placid to buy new skates. Bill is of the same breed as Buddy and his cohorts. And then there is Oovie, a bike rider, speed skater and good friend of Bud's, who with his German accent is an expert on everything.

These gentlemen may be different from one another but they have one thing in common. They skate one helluva lot better than I do.

Post Script

I continued to skate for a year but eventually hung up my skates (the new ones I had just bought) as I would take an occasional spill and despite all my padding, that ice is hard. I was quite literally stumbling.

CARS, CARS AND MORE CARS

What would we do without them?

"Hi there, my name is Nate. How can I help you today?"
"I'm looking to buy a new car and your Civic is one of the cars I'm interested in." And so it went– a test drive, discuss prices, go home to review prices on the Internet, then back to the dealer a week later for final negotiations and an eventual sale.

It was not always like that. Let me tell you my story – probably typical for someone my age (74) but I think it worth telling.

The first car

The year was 1950 and I was 18 years old - old enough to drink but could not see well enough to pass the eye test for a driver's license. Billy Quill could see OK but at 17 was not old enough to drink. It was a symbiotic match made in heaven (or Rosedale anyway). Billy took my eye test and I got him a duplicate of my draft card. He could now drink and I could now drive as well as drink. I could even own a car.

That first car was a 1937 Chrysler with Chinese red window frames. Mattie Fay and I chipped in $5 each to buy this piece of junk – the first of many heaps I owned over the years. Insurance was not required and we certainly could not afford it. We got a ticket for not having a red tail light, paid a $7 fine and repaired it with red cellophane.

Car number two

The second car was a 1932 Model B Ford bought from Jay Ryan for $50. It was a two-door coupe with a rumble seat. Along with the conventional controls, it had a throttle lever on the steering column. One day while showing off to a young lady how fast it would go, I put my foot to the floor and to get every last ounce of speed I advanced the throttle lever. We were on a nearby abandoned runway strip and as we approached its end I took my foot off the gas and stepped on the brakes – and nothing happened. The car did not slow down. I stamped on the brakes harder but it still did not slow down and now we were off the runway and into high grass heading for a large hedge. Bouncing through the rough terrain and completely befuddled as to why the car would not stop I finally realized the throttle lever was still advanced. That was my first attempt at remaining cool under fire. Did not quite make it. I stumbled.

Then one night outside a local bar, after drinking too many beers, I got in a car-pushing contest with two midgets. These half pints had also consumed too many full pints and we all thought it was real fun trying to push each other's cars. (The cars faced each other bumper to bumper with engines racing and wheels spinning.) I recovered from my hangover but the old Ford suffered terminal injuries from the midget attack. It never was the same and was eventually junked.

The Henry J

I had a thousand dollars when discharged from the army in 1954 and proceeded to use half of it to buy a car – a 1951 Henry J – the absolutely worst car ever built. Henry J. Kaiser had built Liberty ships during the Second World War and produced a freighter from keel laying to completed ship in 30 days. The Henry J, built at a time when there was a high demand for cars must have been built in 30 minutes.

$500 of worthless junk that continually needed repairs. Luckily I had a good friend Bob Rossman, an ace mechanic, who helped me keep it repaired (actually he did most of the work).

I had a minor accident on December 15 1954. It would not have been a big deal except the local newspaper reported it as the only accident that occurred in Floral Park on President Dwight Eisenhower's proclaimed Safe Driving Day.

When Henry J passed away he was followed by a succession of heaps. In one of them I kept a two-gallon can of oil. (Those were the days when station attendants - there was no self serve - would always ask, "Check the oil?" when pumping the gas.) Many cars burned oil, mine drank it and then exhaled huge billows of black smelly smoke.

The first new cars

In 1958 at age 26 I got my first real job. It was as an engineering aide with the Sperry Gyroscope Company. With the real job, I got a real car – a brand new 1959 Plymouth Belvedere. I totaled it a year later (subject of another essay in my memoirs) and bought a 1960 Volkswagen Beetle. It was a well-designed vehicle for its time but the time was 1938 when Adolf Hitler promoted its development as the "Peoples Car". At 36 horsepower it drove OK on flat Long Island but to go over a speed bump required downshifting. Taking it on ski trips to Vermont was great for driving in the snow with the weight of the rear-mounted engine over the drive wheels. However, its speed was reduced to a crawl when climbing a hill. As a further indication of its retro design, there was no gas gauge. When the engine started to sputter a lever was kicked over to get another gallon of gas from the tank. The air-cooled engine also did not provide sufficient heat in the winter and sometimes the windshield would freeze up in extremely cold weather. And this was when it was new. Conditions deteriorated a few years later when my sister Marge drove it into the back of a taxicab. After the repair, the wind would whistle through the glove box essentially adding an unclosed window to the driving experience. Despite it all, this little car had its 15 minutes of fame (actually it was two years) appearing in the official VW brochure in 1968 and 1969. (The picture was taken at Pine Hollow Court with our house in the background.)

Aside: in the 1960's one thousand car miles was equal to about one human year.

At close to 100,000 miles my little red VW just curled up and died of old age. It was replaced with a polar blue 1970 Volkswagen Beetle. It did not look a heck of a lot different from the red one I bought ten years earlier, but it did have a slightly more powerful engine and entering the twentieth century, it now had a gas gauge. When it reached the equivalent of four score and ten human years, it too succumbed to the ravages of old age.

Married with children

As the years rolled on Barbara and I (we married in 1963) had a succession of cars, some old and some new, with the emphasis on the bare bone essentials. A two car family, one of them was always a station wagon (SUV's were just letters in the alphabet and Barbara considered vans unsafe). Although nowadays we would not think of getting a car without air conditioning, our first car with this convenience was in 1976, an eight passenger Chevrolet Impala wagon. (It was stolen five years later.) Recent vehicles have been Toyotas and Hondas and they include all sorts of modern conveniences and safety features.

Years ago I would perform tune-ups that included changing sparkplugs, points and condensers, and adjusting the carburetor. Good thing modern cars are highly reliable as I would sooner perform brain surgery than attempt any maintenance or repair on the current complex machines.

So now every few years I walk into a dealer and say, "I'm looking to buy a new car and.....".

OH SAY CAN YOU SEE

All the wrinkles on me.

There he was, this old guy, with wrinkled face, whisker stubble, and liver spots staring me right in the face. His eyes did not just have crow's feet; his entire mug had been victimized by those little creatures. He looked familiar, but who could it be?

Unfortunately it was me looking out from the bathroom mirror following my regular nocturnal trip to that facility. That was the bad news. The good news? It was the first time in years I had seen so clearly. A little explanation is in order.

Born with poor vision in one eye and normal vision in the other, I have managed to live an active life, with only a few difficulties. Sports involving small balls (tennis, baseball and the like) were difficult to judge because of a lack of three-dimensional vision, and many a ball bounced off my head before I realized these games were not for me. However, I played lots of basketball (height was my main problem not vision) and have been involved in many active sports. I had someone take my eye test for a driver's license (only vision in one eye is required nowadays), took flying lessons (same requirement), and was in the paratroopers (two good eyes required but somehow it was overlooked).

162

The lens implant

Then this past summer (2007) a thin veil was beginning to cloud my vision. Maybe I was under the spell of Lamont Cranston (The Shadow) who had the ability to cloud men's minds, since the details of life around me were gradually disappearing. In actuality, however, I was told a few years earlier that through the normal process of aging, cataracts were forming and someday I might need a lens implant in the good eye. This past summer "someday" had arrived.

After a visit to Dr. Krawitz confirmed it was not Lamont's doing, my procedure was scheduled. Although in the medical center for four hours, the actual implant only took a few minutes.

Here is a brief outline of the procedure:

- Jell and drops in eye to numb it and dilate pupil
- IV inserted into back of hand for mild sedation during procedure
- Walk into operating room and lay on table
- IV activated but remain fully conscious and aware of procedure
- One tenth inch incision made in eye and small probe inserted
- Probe breaks up cataract lens and then vacuums it out
- Rolled up quarter inch plastic lens inserted into incision
- Lens unrolled and put into place
- Get up and walk out of operating room

Total time in operating room – 15 minutes. No blood, no stitches, no bandages.

That evening I watched some of the World Series and did some reading but my vision was blurry and I wondered if the operation was a success – after all it was performed over six hours earlier. I went to bed wondering if I would ever see normally again. Then I woke up in the middle of the night and looked in the mirror.

My vision has taken on a new dimension. Although it is still not 3-D, colors are vivid, newsprint looks like the press was just inked, and the world has taken on new clarity. One more miracle of modern medicine!

THE MUSIC MAN

Music has been a family tradition.

Stare, think, plunk. Stare, think, plunk. I am practicing the piano – taking a fairly simple, but lively tune that when played by me sounds more like a slow ponderous funeral dirge. There is a reason. It takes a while to figure out what keys on the piano correspond to those little spots on the sheet music. But that is now. A little of my musical background is in order.

Juilliard School

My mother, Marion, graduated from the Juilliard School in the late 1920s majoring in piano. She had come to New York from Idaho with her mother to attend the school. My father, Ralph, who arrived in New York in 1919, via Ellis Island was an engineer by profession but was accomplished on the violin. (How accomplished, I am not sure. I thought he was very good, my sister, Marge questioned it.) Genetically speaking you might say I had a predisposition to having musical talent. But, you all know about mutant genes.

Early piano lessons

At the age of seven I started piano lessons. As with school, the army and many other things in life I did not enjoy it. Practice was boring, the pieces were simplified versions of the classics, that I detested, and I watched the clock as much as I did the music. My teacher was a young Jewish woman who lived around the block and would walk to our little Cape Cod home once each week for my lesson. I say Jewish because for the first time in my life I heard the expression, "Christ killer". I overheard her telling my father someone had recently called her that. Intolerance has not changed over the years it has just been redirected. But I digress.

For the next five years I diligently, if not enthusiastically, took my lessons and practiced. Rimsky-Korsakov's, Flight of the Bumble Bee was my masterpiece, played with flashing fingers and sounding not bad. Unfortunately, that was the culmination of my youthful musical training. A succession of discordant family crises along with a lack of personal interest ended my piano playing for the next six decades.

Musical aside: Whatever melodious DNA I missed surely went to my sister. She learned to play the piano and guitar, and she could sing – really sing. To me she sounded like Patsy Cline. With her guitar, she could entertain for hours. She also sang in a barbershop quartet and for practice would sing separately all four parts of the harmony.

The guitar

There was no further musical interest until I met Harvey Sherman. I was in my late twenties, an engineer with the Sperry Gyroscope Company and a new member of the Sperry Ski Club. Harvey, a skier, was personable, outgoing and the supreme egotist. He thought he could really play the guitar although he only knew just three chords – C, D7 and G. He had a pleasant voice, knew the words to a few tired old folk songs (On Top of Old Smoky, Tom Dooley), but more than anything he had chutzpah. Lots of it. He would even write poetry to the girls. He showed me one – "An Ode to Gail". There were other poems, same words different names. He said they really worked. What a guy! Everything I was not.

My musical interest returned. I bought a cheap guitar, had Harvey show me his three chords and was now back in the music business. Over the next few years I learned a few more chords, a few more tunes and thought I was pretty good. However, the girls did not flock to me as they did to Harvey. Maybe I was not so good, or maybe I just was not Harvey. However, I was not ready to write poetry.

After getting married, my wife, three kids, home and job pre-empted any guitar plunking. I also did not have a hell of a lot of talent. We did get a piano from Barbara's folks that Bobbi took lessons on and over the years I would occasionally think about taking them. To test my discipline prior to making any decision I would try to practice regularly. It would last a week or so, then I would lose patience and realize I was not ready for lessons.

Piano reprise

At age 73, I thought I would try again. Took out some old sheet music and music books that were in the piano bench and willed myself to practice one half hour each day. I managed to stay marginally interested but did not think it would last. Then, Carol Howell, a good friend and accomplished pianist told me of a simplified technique, using just chords in the left hand and a single melody line of notes in the right. I have tried it and it works. Instant gratification is what is needed at my age. (It is almost like Professor Harold Hill's "Think System". Remember him from "Music Man"?) Maybe eventually I will be able to play some tunes at a brisker pace and without too many clunkers.

Now back to practice. Stare, think, plunk. Stare, think, plunk.

Post script

I did eventually take formal piano lessons but basically using the same technique

FLORIDA

Land of sunshine, but I prefer Long Island (except in the middle of winter).

In 1513, Ponce de Leon was the first white man to set foot in the state of Florida. He was searching for the fountain of youth. In 1954, recently discharged from the U.S. Army, I ventured forth into this same land searching for a different kind of youth – the female variety. He arrived in St. Augustine by boat. I arrived in Fort Lauderdale via Bob Martin's chartreuse Ford convertible. Neither Ponce nor I found what we were looking for.

In 1960 I again ventured to the land of sunshine. It was to Cape Canaveral (changed in 1963 to Cape Kennedy and then back to Cape Canaveral in 1973) where as a young engineer for the Sperry Gyroscope Company my job was to evaluate performance data from a submarine being tested off the Cape - the SSB(N) 598 George Washington. It was the first nuclear submarine outfitted with Polaris intercontinental ballistic missiles capable of annihilating most of Russia's major cities. This was during the Cold War stalemate with the Soviet Union, where the basic strategy was that neither country would start a nuclear war because of immediate complete destructive retaliation. The strategy was called MAD (mutually assured destruction). I found it ironic to be working on something that would only be considered successful if it was never used.

The kayak

I was there for six weeks and had a fair amount of free time, especially on the weekends. So I bought a Pioneer collapsible canvas kayak. However, it was not your ordinary run-of-the-mill kayak. This vessel was also a ketch rigged sailboat with two masts, three sails, two leeboards (in lieu of a centerboard), and a foot controlled steerable rudder. It was also fully collapsible with all parts stored in three easily transported canvas bags that could be assembled by a child in 20 minutes. So the advertisements said.

It was shipped to my motel where I assembled it in my room. It took four hours to connect all those parts and it took the motel cleaning staff an equal amount of time to remove all the packing material embedded in the rug (most of it was loose straw). I never could put that thing together in less than an hour and although it was OK as a kayak it sailed the way you would expect a two-masted, three-sailed, two lee-boarded kayak would sail. Terribly. However, I did spend quite a few enjoyable hours sailing and paddling on the nearby Banana River.

Return visits

Over the years I have been back to the land of alligators a number of times. Once to Marco Island following by-pass surgery in 1994 and a few years later in search of property, either waterfront or on a golf course. The Internet had indicated yes I could afford it, looking at real properties and market prices convinced me otherwise.

Unless you were an astute Florida real estate investor many years back (which I was not), reasonably wealthy (which I am not) or willing to live away from the water (which I am also not) then Florida is a place to visit, not to live. However even visiting poses its problems. If you don't stay at an expensive location right on the water, chances are you wouldn't even know it was there; a wall of high-rises line the shore. There are few beach access points and where there are, the parking is limited. (Robert Moses, why didn't you exercise your dictatorial building plans in this lovely state? Miami Beach State Park has such a lovely ring to it.)

I must speak of traffic. A one-word description is – abomination. Multi-lane roads with left and right turning lanes, and computerized traffic signals are all used to speed traffic along. However, there are just too many people with too many cars. Everybody and their sister want to live and vacation in this warm climate and along the shore. But there is only so much shore, then there is no more!

So I visit Florida (most recently Sanibel Island), pay lots of money for a place on the water, enjoy it for a week, then head back home to the cold, damp, crummy winter weather of Long Island. But it is my cold, damp, crummy weather and it is my home.

BIKE RIDES ACROSS IOWA

It is not flat.

Frank Springer and I making ritual rear wheel dip in Missouri River at start of ride

To explain the origin of this adventure requires a brief step back in time. In 1992 Frank Springer, Greenlawn neighbor, good friend, fellow jogger and bike rider, read a New York Times article about a 500 mile, one week long, bike ride across the state of Iowa. It was an annual ritual started by the Des Moines Register (a statewide newspaper) in 1972 that had grown into an annual event taking place the last full week in July each year. It was called RAGBRAI (Register's Annual Great Bike Ride Across Iowa) and Frank asked if I wanted to join him.

"Where will you stay at night?"

"In a tent"

"What is the weather like?"

"Humid and in the nineties?

"What happens when it rains?"

"What do you think?"

"Frank, I think I'll pass"

Frank went; I stayed home. He confirmed all his answers to me and then went again the next year. I stayed home, but started thinking, maybe there was something to RAGBRAI that could not be easily defined.

Finally, in 1995 I decided to join Frank on his annual trek across Iowa. (I was not even sure where Iowa was. Was there a city named Boise there? No that is in Idaho, wherever that is.) Also, what I hadn't realized was that RAGBRAI was an exclusive event – only 10,000 riders could be accepted. Only 10,000? I did not think there were that many masochists looking to abuse their bodies in 90+-degree weather, rain or shine for seven straight days, and sleep in tiny tents on the hard ground for seven straight nights. Not to mention the logistics in getting the bike safely packed and shipped to Iowa, and arranging to coordinate flights to and from the middle of nowhere. But more than 10,000 apply each year and only the lucky ones are rejected (only kidding). Frank and I made the lottery and would be riding with a support group called Pork Belly Ventures (PBV) run by Tammy Pavitch and her brother Pete Phillips. (They had a large Ryder truck into which each morning we would load our camping gear and then meet them later at that day's destination town.) How PBV got its name I don't know, but each year they provided support for about 150 riders and would bring along a baby porker as a mascot. If you were inclined to pick up that little piglet you would instantly know where the expression "squealed like a stuck pig" came from (and he was not even stuck). You might also discover, as Frank did, they are not toilet trained.

In early July, we shipped our bikes to Pete who then met us at Eppley Airfield in Omaha, Nebraska on the Friday night preceding the Sunday start. He drove us to a motel in Council Bluffs, Iowa, just a short ride on the other side of the Missouri River. The next day we were taken to the RAGBRAI start in Onowa - a different town each year but always on the western border of the state along the Missouri River. The ride always starts with a ritual dip of the rear wheel in this river and this is done on Saturday. The official ride starts the next morning and ends the following Saturday with the front wheel dipped in the Mississippi River.

The Route

Each January the Des Moines Register announces the RAGBRAI route for the coming July. The route - always different - takes 10,000 bikers and accompanying families through small towns separated by miles of cornfields and occasional pig farms. (The never-ending rolling fields of corn remain memorable images. Riding by the pig farms I just remember holding my nose.) Since RAGBRAI is always the last full week in July, this guarantees it will be hot and humid – ideal for growing corn, not so ideal for bikers pedaling 80 miles a day over the rolling hills of our country's heartland. (Contrary to popular belief, Iowa is not flat.)

Each day we typically bike through at least five small towns (some with populations of 150 or less) and then stay overnight at a locale that can accommodate a fivefold increase in population. Most towns vie for inclusion in the route as it is a means of making a few dollars and adds a little excitement to a pleasant but humdrum life style. These towns start preparing for their few hours of fame right after the January route announcement.

The pass-through towns that sit quietly 364 days of the year must be ready to handle the swarm of hot, sweaty, thirsty, hungry bikers that for a few hours on one hot July day will be the insatiable consumers of vast quantities of beer, soda, bottled water and food. They are also in the market for souvenirs, tee shirts and other mementos of their adventure. There is money to be made!

To be on the RAGBRAI route, towns are required to provide some form of entertainment and as a minimum they set up a bandstand on their Main Street with a local group blasting out music on an over-amplified sound system. This is augmented with anything from the town mayor telling jokes, to Elvis impersonators, singing nuns, country singers and the ersatz Blues Brothers. Bikers contribute with street dancing, limbo contests, beer drinking binges and the other excesses of exuberant youth (viewed and thoroughly enjoyed by us more mature voyeurs).

The stopover towns, which are more than just crossroad farm communities must accommodate the many thousands of bikers with their tents, campers and appetites. Public parks, high school fields and local folk's front yards provide impromptu campgrounds. Where available, college campuses and airstrips (takeoffs and landings suspended for the day) are also used. Hundreds of portable lavatories (called kybos) have to be provided along with shower facilities, food tents, church suppers, and local transportation (bikers, weary from a day in the saddle don't feel the need for additional exercise). All this for a brief overnight stay. And it might be years before another RAGBRAI event passes through this same town.

I made the ride five successive years starting in 1995. Sometimes with Frank and sometimes with others. The following is a composite from notes and diaries I kept over those years.

The Ride

The day starts early, at about 5 AM, an hour before sunup. We quickly dress, then jam tents, sleeping bags and all our other gear into a single duffle bag and load it onto the Pork Bellies truck. An early start allows a ride that at least begins during the coolest part of the day. As we mount our bikes, the sun is just peeking above the horizon and it creates huge elongated shadows on the road that are fascinating to watch as we ride. After about an hour we stop for breakfast – usually with the Pancake Man or Chris Cakes, who have set up in a local farmer's barn, firehouse or makeshift tent. No matter where, it is always interesting, entertaining, tasty - and a bargain. The griddles are right out of Ripley's Believe it or Not, at 30 feet long with a device about a foot above it that travels on a track dropping four blobs of pancake batter every foot along the way. Long lines move quickly as this marvelous machine spews forth its pancakes by the hundreds. When being served we might be asked to step back about ten feet and catch our serving as it is tossed from the grill. Not all are caught, to the delight of those waiting in line. A stack of cakes plus sausage, juice and coffee is $3.50. Of course we might have to eat outside, maybe standing up, and if it is raining – get wet. But this is RAGBRAI.

Although some days would be tiring - they were always interesting. The local Iowans were always friendly and when there are 10,000 bikers traveling in an army across the state there are always some wacky remembrances.

Diary entry

Today we rode through the towns of Melvin and George and bypassed Edna. Strange names. Saw a bicycle built for four and team Wedgie. Also saw a rider wearing a Stetson, towing a small trailer. On the trailer – a boom box blasting rock music along with a tiny Scottie wearing sunglasses.

Diary entry

In the afternoon we stopped in the Czech town of Spillville where Anton Dvorak spent the summer of 1893. In the house where he stayed there was also the Bily Clock Museum. However, today the few that entered were more interested in the air conditioning than anything else. Price for about one hour of cool air; $3.50.

Diary entry

Frank stood on the second floor of a gazebo in the town park and announced that if elected mayor he would eliminate all taxes. Got a few laughs and some odd stares. At our next stop there was a limbo contest going on in the middle of the town's main street and some of the RAGBRAI participants were quite good. I could not crawl as low as some of the folks in this competition.

In Winterset we rode by the house where "Duke" Wayne was born. Many think of him as a hero because of the roles he played in the movies. To me he was just a WWII draft dodger. We biked through the bridges of "Bridges of Madison County" book and movie fame, and in West Bend we visited the Grotto of the Redemption advertised as the "Eighth Wonder of the World". I wondered eight times why anybody would build something so ugly and grotesque. But who am I to judge? The structure was elaborate and I guess it is an article of faith to the people who built and maintain it.

At Steamboat Rock, while walking in town amidst thousands of slowly riding bikers a woman in front of me fell off her bike. In trying to avoid her, I fell and scraped my arm - my war wound for the week. I was very proud of it and tried to keep the bruise festering, but it completely healed by the time I got home.

Although ninety percent of Iowa's economy is agriculture there is nothing like the tourist industry for a few short days in July. The Four-H Club, Girl Scouts, Boy Scouts, Rotaries, and once-a-year entrepreneurs, are all out on the side of these normally deserted farm roads selling pancakes, hot dogs, smoothies, water, soda and even root beer floats.

Diary entry

Today was to be the longest ride of the week, 92 miles, so we tried to put in a fair amount of distance before stopping for breakfast. We therefore missed our usual pancakes and after 30 miles stopped in the little town of Jesup for funnel cakes. These are fried pastry served with powdered sugar and are tasty but definitely artery clogging.

Diary entry

*Our next stop was Mr. Porkchop (a RAGBRAI traditional vendor who cooks delicious pork chops - using corncobs for fuel - and sits on the side of the road bellowing **PORRRRK CHOPPPPPPPS**). Andy had a $5.00 pork chop and it was eaten while standing as there are not too many chairs on RAGBRAI (to be exact – none).*

We would usually arrive at the day's destination town in early afternoon where 10,000 bikers were all trying to find where they were staying. Little posters were tacked up on trees and telephone poles with arrows leading to the campsites of the many different groups. We would look for the smiling PBV pig face with his arrow. That is the direction we would point our bikes.

Diary entry

Our campsite was in a park next to the swimming pool, close to the kybos and near the food vendors. It was a veritable RAGBRAI heaven. There was a long line for the showers at the pool, but there happened to be a hose nearby that allowed the less inhibited to quickly shower (more about that later) and then enjoy the pool - which also had a great slide.

Frank and I walked to the nearby food vendors for an evening of outdoor dining on junk food. We met a hobo who wrote poetry about trains and Frank expounded on F.D.R., Maine, Iowa (its size, agricultural output and so on). Since we were running low on clean clothes, we bought two of last year's RAGBRAI tee shirts at $5 apiece.

Although it usually does not rain much this time of year, there was always the threat of tornadoes. Signs were posted at the campsites stating the nearest shelter. Not all were solid buildings. I remember one sign pointing to the bottom of a bramble covered ravine.

Diary entry

At about 11 PM the police came through with bullhorns announcing, "Severe weather will hit the area in 25 minutes. Take shelter immediately". Many people went to a bus barn adjoining the campground and other campers sought shelter in nearby buildings. I was just too tired to move so I brought my bike inside the tent to provide a little more ballast and decided to wait it out. Right on schedule the storm hit with spectacular flashes of lightning illuminating the sky and moving directly at us. As it moved through the campsite, a bolt of lightning (with a simultaneous crack of thunder) hit close by. The winds picked up and for a few moments I was sure some of the tents would be heading for the Land of Oz. I quickly put on my bike helmet, leaned against the windward side of the tent and grabbed the tent poles in an attempt to prevent a disaster. However, the high winds only lasted a short time and the rain settled down to a steady downpour.

After a long hot day's ride, showers were sometimes available in the local high school or municipal pool, but usually required taking a shuttle bus and then waiting in a long line. However, there were other ways to remove the blood, sweat and tears from our tired aching bodies.

One evening showers were in the Clear Lake Community Bus Garage. Four 60-foot long overhead pipes, each with 20 showerheads, had been temporarily installed to provide a mass production solution. Main complaint? The clogged drain caused everyone to shower in ankle deep dirty water.

Car washes were temporarily converted for use as showers, with the standard joke, "I'll also take a full body wax job". No, you did not get pulled through high-pressure soap and rinse sprays, and get scrubbed by huge rotating brushes. Hoses hung from the ceiling and for about a dollar, reasonable showers were obtained.

As there is an alternative approach to medicine, there is also an alternative approach to showering.

Diary entry

Our campsite was at the local airport next to the runway and out in the hot sun. A nearby garden hose provided the shower facilities for those of us unwilling to use the more conventional facilities (this required a bus ride and a long wait). Coed hose showers require a special technique; (1) wet yourself and discretely shove the hose in your bathing suit to include all body parts, (2) hand the hose to the next person and then lather yourself, discretely turning away to include the entire body, (3) upon receiving the hose again rinse thoroughly using the same technique as in (1). The water is invariably cold, but the pressure is high and an acceptable body cleansing is possible if one is not inhibited. It really is much more convenient than the car wash.

Dinner varied. It might be an all you can eat church supper or a couple of hot dogs from a local vendor. Entertainment also varied. It could be a walk through town, listen to guitar playing from a couple of talented NYC firefighters (one later died in the 9/11 attack), or just sit around and swap stories.

Diary entry

Andy, Art and I took the shuttle bus to town for a lasagna dinner at the Knights of Columbus. We ate huge amounts of food that tasted absolutely delicious; it happens when you are famished. In the middle of town there was a 30-foot high inflatable model of a sinking Titanic. It provided a slide down the sloping deck for those willing to pay a dollar and walk up 30 feet of stairs. There was a men's chorus singing gospels on a side street and a juggler on a unicycle performing in the middle of the street. Also, a large screen was set up for a laser show that was to be performed later that night. But we were ready for the sack; it was 9 PM.

By Saturday, day seven, we are really weary and looking forward to the ride's end. But when it is all over I look back and tend to just remember the good aspects of RAGBRAI.

Diary entry

Although the ride was the hilliest of the week, it was a day that would insure that I left Iowa with pleasant memories and the desire for another return next year. The scenery was out of a picture book - rolling hills covered with fields of soybeans and corn, with farmhouses and silos in the distance. The views couldn't be captured by a camera even though many tried.

We arrived at our final destination Sabula (a small island town in the Mississippi River) at 2 PM, made the ritual front wheel dip into the river and then started the frantic process of preparing to leave. There were literally thousands of bikers trying to connect with their charter groups, friends, buses, trucks and cars in order to head for home. In addition, the main street was filled with vendors trying to sell their remaining RAGBRAI XXVII products. We packed our bikes in beat up boxes padded with dirty clothes and took them via PBV pickup truck to the UPS station for shipment home.

When done, Frank and I boarded our charter bus for the seven-hour trip back to Council Bluffs where we would stay overnight in a motel with a bed and flush toilet, and fly home the next day.

No more hose showers for at least another year.

Trip end with ritual front wheel dip in Mississippi

THE TRIATHLON

Silver Threads Among the Gold

I n the Vytra-Tobay Triathlon swimmers go of in groups or waves of 100 people at intervals of four minutes. Each wave has a different color bathing cap and my wife Barbara noticed that in past triathlons when completing the swim, my cap was always a different color then those swimmers around me. If the yellow caps werc three or four waves after me, my white cap would be surrounded by them at the end – if they hadn't already passed me. That is the metaphor of my life. I manage to finish but always seem to be a little late. High school, college, getting a decent job, getting married and having grandchildren – always a little late. But back to the 2005 triathlon.

It was a hot August morning with temperatures that would eventually go into the high 90s. The one-kilometer (.62 mile) swim was actually .8 miles and it took me close to one hour (official time 55 minutes 44 seconds) to finish that first of three legs of the race. Where most people leave the water running toward their bicycles, I stumbled toward mine, slowly put on my sneakers and bike helmet, and then – with legs that felt like lead - started to ride. The one short but steep hill on the course had never caused me trouble before, but this time it felt like pedaling up Pike's Peak. I had to dismount half way up and even walking was difficult. Since the bike course ends with a nearly three mile downhill ride into Oyster Bay I thought it would allow my legs to rest up for the three mile run - the first half of which is up some very steep hills. *I thought wrong.*

After getting off the bike I started the arduous task of trying to look like I was jogging. But I was truly out of gas and only managed to shuffle a few steps past the starting line before breaking into a walk – and not a very fast one at that. And the hills hadn't even started yet. Then my calf muscles started to tighten and I wondered if I would be able to finish. After what seemed an endless ordeal (with a little slow jogging on the downhills) I eventually approached the finish. Most participants had completed the triathlon by this time and there were not many spectators left to applaud my late arrival. However my son, Stephen, and my co-favorite grandsons, Ray and Will, gave me a rousing cheer as I stumbled across the finish line two and a half hours after my silver cap (actually white) had entered the water.

The good news was that when awards were presented later that morning I received a plaque for second place in my age category (70 – 74). However it came with a caveat – there was only one other person in my age group and he beat me. More silver threads among the gold.

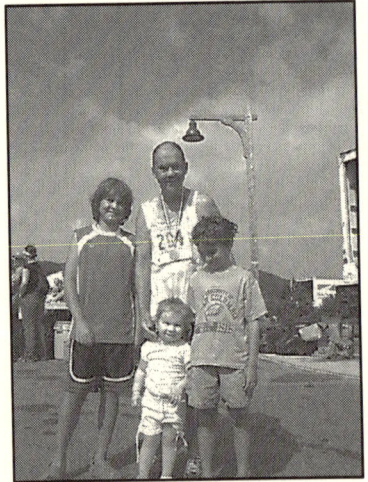

Will, me, Ray and Maddie

Made in the USA
Charleston, SC
20 January 2014